JOURNEY into COMPASSION

A Spirituality for the Long Haul

JAMES McGINNIS

ORBIS BOOKS

Maryknoll, New York 10545

The Catholic Foreign Mission Society of America (Maryknoll) recruits and trains people for overseas missionary service. Through Orbis Books, Maryknoll aims to foster the international dialogue that is essential to mission. The books published, however, reflect the opinions of their authors and are not meant to represent the official position of the society.

Published in the United States by Orbis Books, Maryknoll, NY 10545

Originally published by The Crossroad Publishing Company, 370 Lexington Ave., New York, NY 10017 and The Institute for Peace and Justice, 4144 Lindell Blvd., #122, St. Louis, MO 63108

Manufactured in the United States of America

ORBIS/ISBN 0-88344-926-9

Contents

Foreword, *Richard Rohr, O.F.M.*   v

Preface   vii

1 Be Not Afraid   1

2 A Dream for the Journey   9

3 The Power of Suffering Love   20

4 Peacemaking and Prayer   32

5 The Lord's Supper, Our Ultimate Source of Solidarity   45

6 Living on Gospel Terms: A Lifestyle of Solidarity   60

7 Love Is the Measure   75

8 Reconciliation with the Earth   90

9 "Love Your Mother, Work for Peace"   104

10 Solidarity as Resistance   114

11 Accepting and Testing Our Limits   128

Notes

Foreword

AFTER GIVING RETREATS of many types for twenty years, I am aware of the need, the possibilities, the desire for this kind of book. Again and again, people of tremendous good will tell me that "no one ever told me that before." We are not aware that most of our educational endeavors still assume and accept the middle-class American worldview. It is still the only reference point and perspective for most of our people. Church, Gospel, kingdom values, have not been presented as a real alternative vision of society, but merely a way of being "religious" within the existing and unquestioned society.

The endless energy and imagination of Jim McGinnis will feed and challenge you on this retreat-adventure. It is a wonderful mixture of both profound depth and utter simplicity. Both the shallow and the sophisticated parts of our souls will be stretched. Jim will be both didactic and inspiring. He will exhaust and excite you as he offers new ways of thinking, new ways of feeling, new ways of doing and acting, new ways of listening, and new ways of belonging. He makes a new lifestyle both possible and touchable. It sounds like conversion, but a conversion that is now realistic instead of wished for, talked about, and guilt-ridden. Jim's practical steps and gestures take a lot of the paralysis out of the merely preached and hard-to-hear Gospel. Most of us are doers and we need to make concrete decisions, carry out specific actions, and experience at least a little bit of change — in ourselves and in the world.

Yet we know that we are first of all not talking about success, but about spirituality. We want our lives to make a difference on this suffering planet, but first of all we want our lives themselves to be different. Jim's own spiritual journeys will be a strong witness to the primacy of inner surrender, quiet, harmony, and detachment. These essential lessons are not learned from books (even this one!), but by making journeys of faith ourselves. We have to plant ourselves in places and circumstances where the old answers don't work anymore. In that precarious position, God gets both real and dangerous. I don't think that conversion happens in any other way. Most of us are just not smart enough or heroic enough to walk headlong into Gospel freedom. As you might expect, Dorothy Day put it well when she said that she wanted to live so close to the bottom that when the system fell apart, she would not have far to fall. I think that is about as good a description of biblical faith as we are likely to come across. Much of the rest is religious jargon and jingoism.

I am grateful that we are moving beyond words to action. It is a much better teacher, precisely because we make mistakes, reveal our shadow self, and awaken our deepest inner resources of power and patience. This spirituality is not for navel-gazers or mind-trippers, but for people who want to put the inner and outer life together in one honest place. Spirit, after all, is not the opposite of worldly matter, but Spirit is that divine capacity to hold all disparate matter together in perfect balance and harmony.

May this Spirit-filled book — and your ensuing journey — be another gracious link in the movement toward that harmony.

Richard Rohr, O.F.M.
Center for Action and Contemplation
Albuquerque, New Mexico

Preface

BECAUSE THIS WILL PROBABLY BE a reading experience different from what you are used to, there are a number of things I need to tell you before we get started. First, I envision this book as a retreat we are making together, so I'm writing this as a personal conversation with you. Although I cannot hear your responses as you read, I will try to anticipate your concerns, questions, and feelings. I wrote this book with several very specific people in mind, people at different points in their faith journey as they relate to peacemaking. Because I have kept them in mind, I hope I have guessed right at least most of the time when I pause in the text and ask you a question or identify with how I think you might be feeling at that moment. If I guess wrong, I hope you will be patient with me.

I am writing this way for several reasons. First, this is such a personal topic—our faith journeys into peacemaking and discipleship. I don't know any other way to be true to myself than to speak in personal terms and think of you quite personally. Second, I am more comfortable as a speaker than as a writer. I like an informal dialogue style. Third, I want you to interact with what I write. So I ask questions or ask you to stop and reflect on what I have written before you go on. Sometimes the questions are at the point where an issue is discussed in the text; other times I save them for the end of the chapter. Use them and all my directions *as you see fit*. Do not feel compelled to follow my lead if my questions or directions are not appropriate. Use what I write in the way most conducive to your own style and pace.

Who do I think you are? I am writing for people who sense that they are on a faith journey. I think your faith is important to you, that you sense a connection between your faith life and your concern for the well-being of others. Worship and prayer are important for you; otherwise you would not be interested in this book. And you have some sense of being on a journey. I believe that you sense God working in your life, leading you in some way, and that you have already taken many steps on that journey.

As a Christian myself, I am writing primarily—but not exclusively—for fellow Christians. I write in explicitly Christian terms, speaking of Jesus very directly, because Jesus is central in my life. I don't apologize for my Christian faith, nor do I pretend that I am not a Roman Catholic. I cite the prophetic documents of my own church and other Christian churches, not because I think they are more "right" than other faith statements. They are ones that have etched themselves into my soul. But others have too and I hope I am an "inclusive" Christian. I have had many beautiful interfaith experiences and relationships, and I hope to share some of that richness with you. I quote from a variety of faith traditions, with special emphasis on the Hebrew prophets and the contemporary Hindu prophet, Gandhi. Both have been an integral part of my faith journey. Jewish friends suggested that I use "Adonai" instead of "Yahweh" when quoting from the Hebrew prophets, because "Adonai" is the more intimate term for God. I hope that people of Jewish, Muslim, Hindu, Buddhist, Baha'i, and other faith traditions read this too.

Two more notes on inclusiveness relate to my frequent use of the phrase "God's Kingdom of Shalom." I think of God and refer to God in both masculine and feminine terms. I realize that "Kingdom" is a male and hierarchical term, but at the time of my first writing I had not yet found a better one. Some people had suggested "Reign," but that doesn't suggest "community," which is so central to "Shalom." Because of that, I now prefer Martin Luther King's phrase, "the beloved community." So I hope you will not be put off by my use of either "Kingdom" or "Father, Mother, Creator God." Likewise, as someone raised on the Jewish and Christian Scriptures, I know of no other term that so richly expresses the fullness of what God has in store for us and the whole of creation than "Shalom." But I am also aware that to some Arab Christians and people of Islamic faith, "Shalom" has political connotations that are very painful. I want to be more sensitive to that pain and more willing to work for justice and peace for all peoples of the Middle East. At the same time, I want to be as true to the richness of the faith tradition of the primary readers of this book. Consequently, I use "Shalom" to encompass the unity, harmony, integrity, and material well-being that is the essence of what I believe is God's plan and promise for creation.

A little more about myself. I was born in 1942, so my faith journey is in its middle years. I have come a long way, thanks to many people through whom God's grace has been abundantly shared with me, and I have a long way to go. I have been married for over twenty-five years to a wonderful woman named Kathy McCoy. At this writing, we have three very typical and absolutely unique young adult children—Tom (twenty-two), David (twenty), and Theresa (eighteen). If you are a parent or care for children in other ways, you may find some special help in what follows. My faith journey definitely includes my life as husband and father.

In terms of career, I have been working for peace and justice full-time for twenty-five years, primarily as an educator. I don't think that is the case with most of you. But that shouldn't make any difference. I see all of us as peacemakers and prophets, whether we do it full-time or part-time. My faith journey has taken me to a number of countries and situations that have provided moments of special insight and solidarity. I share many of them, not to impress you or suggest that you do similar things or go similar places. They are the specifics of my journey. If my journey is to be helpful to you, it has to be concrete. I believe strongly in the need for us to share our faith journeys with one another. We need to encourage one another, edify one another, reveal to one another that God is truly acting not only in our own lives but in the world around us.

Because I want this book to inspire you and lead you beyond itself, I have chosen to share some of the faith journey of other peacemakers and prophets. Some I quote at length in hopes you will be inspired by them and want to read more of their works. These are people who have been important to me on my journey and I think should be helpful on yours as well. Most have been men: for example, Gandhi, Francis of Assisi, and Jim Douglass (especially Jim's new book *The Nonviolent Coming of God*, Orbis, 1992). But more and more lately I am finding myself nurtured by feminine sources and working to develop the feminine side of my person.

I refer to specific actions, groups, and resources as a way of enabling you on your journey. I want you to have possibilities always before you. If I think names and addresses will help, then I provide them.[1]* (Endnote numbers in the text followed by an asterisk indicate notes that have special additional information along these lines.)

I would appreciate hearing from you if you have any suggestions for changes in what I have written. I give retreats and days of recollection and am always looking for ways to improve both the content and the process of these experiences.[2]* Many readers of the first edition took me up on this offer, so I hope you do too.

A word of thanks to the special "soul brothers" and "soul sisters" who have accompanied me on my journey and offered suggestions for preliminary drafts. These include Kathy McCoy McGinnis, Richard Rohr, OFM, and Jean Chapman, especially; also Mary Hengen, Mary Lou Kownacki, OSB, Bob Hull, Rev. Joanne Robbins, Jim Rice, Rev. Buck Jones, Jim and Shelley Douglass, Rabbi Jim Goodman, Kass Dotterweich, Tim Cimino, Ron Dart, Pat McCullough, Mary Jo and Jim Brauner.

And special thanks to Bob Gormley and Robert Ellsberg at Orbis Books for extending the life of this book and giving me a chance to update its context and content. Much has happened between 1989 and 1993 to alter our world and our world views.

The dismantling of the Berlin Wall and the dissolution of the Soviet Union have dramatically changed East-West realities. But Chapter 9 on turning enemies into friends and other references to U.S.-Soviet friendship are not out-of-date even though some language changes are necessary. While we may no longer think of Russians and other former members of the Soviet Union as enemies, they remain at least strangers to most of us and hungry ones besides. The barriers between us still need to be broken down. Compassionate outreach in their very difficult time of transition to some new social, political, economic reality seems clearly called for. And while the nuclear arms race has been slowed and even reversed a little, militarism is still alive and well, challenging us on several levels, as Chapter 10 points out. U.S. wars in Panama and the Persian Gulf unmask the persistent presence of militarism—that societal determination to use massive violence to remain on top, in charge, number one. This sinfulness infects us personally as it infects U.S. foreign and domestic policy. The new political administration in Washington is no less susceptible to this sinfulness than previous ones. And there are still "enemies" out there to be reconciled with. Innocent Iraqis and others at home as well as abroad continue to suffer greatly because we as a society cling to our privileges and the ways of domination and retaliation. Our national way of life as well as our individual ways of life still need to be challenged.

The "Earth Summit" in Brazil in June 1992 has further revealed this truth. Chapter 8 on "Reconciliation with the Earth" is even more imperative now than in 1989. A recent report from over 1500 renowned researchers from around the world gives us this decade and not much more, to turn our lives around if we want our planet, our home, our "mother," to survive.

But the biggest change I have experienced since 1989 has been in the awareness of the urgent need to address the issues of racial and economic justice. The explosion in Los Angeles in the spring of 1992 was the loudest of a series of "wake-up calls" to people of faith in the U.S. While the whole Quincentenary year of 1992 was an opportunity for many people of faith and religious institutions to re-examine European and U.S. history, repent for the sinful treatment of people of color, and (re)dedicate ourselves to challenging racism and building multiracial communities, the events in Los Angeles focused the need even more. The little that I wrote on racism on pages 123-24 needs to be expanded. The initial steps suggested on those pages should lead us to create multiracial communities wherever we can, no matter how small to start. Out of these relationships will come not only the actions we need to take to address racial and economic justice, but also the courage and accountability and support to carry out these actions.

As I say several times in the chapters that follow, relationships are everything. Our willingness to go more deeply into any issue—whether it's caring for the earth, solidarity with the poor, racism, sexism, or resistance to violence—is dependent on the relationships we have around the issue. We only sacrifice and take risks when we truly care about those (people and the earth herself) involved in the issue.

I see this period of 1992 to the year 2000 as a critical transition period, perhaps the most critical in generations or even centuries, for turning around our lives, our communities, our world. The Chinese word for "crisis" is made up of two characters—

one for "danger" and the other for "opportunity." Truly unique opportunities as well as grave dangers lie before us. With renewed vision and courage, with practical possibilities and companions in the process, we can make a difference.

An expression of vision has been given me in recent years to help carry me into this critical transition period with greater clarity, compassion, and courage and to enrich the vision of unity and diversity, justice and reconciliation, that I share in Chapter 1-3. It is a Native American chant written by Mary Jo Oklesson and recorded by Susan Stark on a wonderful tape named for the chant—*Rainbow People*. I sing it regularly for people of all ages in my workshops and retreats—in sign as well as aloud. I would be happy to send you an essay I did on the theme "We Are a Rainbow People," with the signs as well as the music. The tape is also available from the Institute for Peace and Justice. The chant goes like this:

"We are a rainbow people . . .
"We are beams of golden light . . .
"We are bridges to the dawning of a new day."

"Rainbow People" celebrate the diversity of color in the rainbow and build inclusive lives and communities embracing people of all ages, races, nationalities, genders, levels of ability, sexual orientations, economic classes, and religions. They/we break down barriers and build bridges across all these differences. They/we let our little lights shine and fan the flames of others, making all of us beams of golden light. Jesus is the golden light itself. We are beams of his light. Our fidelity over a lifetime in being a light, a bridge, and part of a rainbow people brings about the dawning of a new day. We don't have to bring the new day to completion. That is the work of Jesus and his Spirit touching faithful people in every generation. We just have to be faithful to our generational moment in this dawning. Perhaps it is 7:15 A.M. The fidelity of our ancestors passed the vision and flame to us at this moment. Our fidelity at 7:15 to passing on the vision and flame to our children will bring the dawning to 7:16. As people of faith, we believe that the high noon of the new day will come. The beloved community will be completed. Our journeys will arrive at the fullness of compassion—Shalom. And I wish you Shalom as you begin your journey through this book.

Chapter 1

Be Not Afraid

WE ARE ON A JOURNEY that stirs both excitement and fear as we face the unknown. God has blessed us to enable us to be at the point in our journeys that we are. We can rejoice in those blessings and celebrate our present point in our journeys. But I also know that I cannot stay where I am at this point. I am reminded of a challenging passage from my own Catholic bishops' pastoral letter, *The Challenge of Peace*: "To be disciples of Jesus requires that we continually go beyond where we are now. To obey the call of Jesus means separating ourselves from all attachments and affiliation that could prevent us from hearing and following our authentic vocation. To set out on the road of discipleship is to dispose oneself for a share in the cross (see John 16:20)." That scares me!

"To set out on the road of discipleship," to choose to write this book or read this book, sounds like we are the ones doing the choosing. We are, but in a deeper sense we are not. We are the chosen more than the choosers. Jesus' words are unambiguous and need to be carved into our souls: "You did not choose me; no, I chose you; and I commissioned you to go out and to bear fruit..." (John 15:16). It is Jesus who calls us daily to follow him on the road of discipleship. He calls us just as he called his first disciples, just as God called the Hebrew prophets. And we are probably just as excited and afraid as they were.

Let's listen to one of those calls, God's call to Jeremiah: "Before I formed you in the womb I knew you; before you came to birth I consecrated you; I have appointed you as prophet to the nations." Jeremiah responded: "Ah, Adonai; look, I do not know how to speak; I am a child!" But Adonai replied: "Do not say, 'I am a child.' Go now to those to whom I send you and say whatever I command you. Do not be afraid of them, for I am with you to protect you — it is Adonai who speaks!" (Jer. 1:6–8).

Most of us can no longer use our "youth" as our excuse, as

1

Jeremiah did, for not wanting to accept God's call, but we all claim not to be experienced enough to be a prophet in our time and place. We are all afraid to be prophets and disciples. Jesus' disciples were terrified, once they realized what was involved. Picture them, the men at least, hovering in fear behind locked doors, soon after Jesus' crucifixion, afraid that what happened to Jesus might happen to them. In no way did they want to lose their lives too! In no way do we want to lose our lives either! And so we find ourselves hovering in fear at times, afraid of where discipleship might lead.

During the Vietnam War years I gradually became convinced of the wrongness of that war and began slowly expressing that conviction. What I remember most were my fears, fears of leafletting on street corners because passers-by might reject me, even make fun of me. I would do anything to avoid leafletting, even though I knew it should be done. Then there were those Saturday mornings once a month when I reported for duty with my National Guard unit. This was during a period of what were called "National Moratorium Days" (1968–1972), when war protestors would wear black arm bands. I felt I should wear my black arm band not only in the safe environment of St. Louis University where I was teaching but also on the drill floor of the National Guard armory where my military police unit met. Faithfully I put the arm band on over my uniform as I dressed at home and was even able to walk into the armory with it on. But by the time of our opening formation, the arm band was off. I was too afraid. I was not willing to risk even that much. I share this, not to suggest that discipleship is to be expressed primarily in leafletting or demonstrations, but to share the brokenness of my response to what I believed was God's call to me to bear prophetic witness. I blew it, to put it bluntly, and did so regularly!

Jesus' Response

So how does Jesus treat us when we blow it? How did he treat his first disciples? They had blown it all. The three he asked to accompany him in the garden of his agony fell asleep as soon as they got there. Hours later Peter, despite his earlier protestations to the contrary, denied Jesus three times. The rest of the men fled, not willing to risk their lives by being seen anywhere near Jesus through his trial, torture, and death. They locked themselves inside a house, hiding out, hoping they would not get caught too. But that Sunday evening Jesus broke through their locked doors and locked hearts and appeared in their midst, saying "Peace be with you." He did not chide them, ask for explanations, or fire them. Rather, he accepted them where they were, with their betrayals, their failures, their fears. He forgave them as he forgives us. And then he sent them forth once more, this time with the promise that the Holy Spirit would accompany them. "The disciples were filled with joy when they saw the Lord, and he said to them again, 'Peace be with you. As the Father sent me, so am I sending you.' After saying this he breathed on them and said, 'Receive the Holy Spirit...'" (John 20:20–22). Pause to reflect on this message, for Jesus is speaking to us as much as he was to his first disciples.

We are offered peace, forgiveness, acceptance for who we are. We are sent forth by a Lord and friend ("I no longer call you servants, but friends" — John 15:15) who understands intimately our fears. He had to wrestle with the same fears. He even sweat blood over those fears. Jesus entered the garden terrified. Twice he begged God to "take this cup away from me" (Mark 14:36–42). Like us, Jesus had to wrestle with his own words. John describes Jesus' struggle after Jesus had gone up to Jerusalem for the last time, knowing that his death was imminent: "Now the hour has come for the Son of Man to be glorified. I tell you, most solemnly, unless a wheat grain falls on the ground and dies, it remains only a single grain; but if it dies, it yields a rich harvest. Anyone who loves his life loses it; anyone who hates his life in this world will keep it for the eternal life. If persons serve me, they must follow me; wherever I am, my servant will be there too. If anyone serves me, my Father will honor him. Now my soul is troubled" (John 12:23–27).

Jesus struggled to the point of sweating blood over whether his death would bear fruit, whether somehow life would prevail, life for himself and for the rest of the world. If he lost his life, would he really find the fullness of life that he had been preaching to others? If this were merely an academic question for someone who already knew the answer, the Gospel writers would not have described Jesus as sweating blood over it. I don't know anyone who has ever sweated blood over anything. I have been very afraid at times, but I have never sweated blood. I take

great comfort realizing that it is this terrified Jesus who calls me
to follow him and who walks with me every step of the way. He
understands my doubts and fears because he experienced them
more than I ever will.

Do We Dare Believe?

Bringing Forth in Hope by Denise Priestly (Paulist Press, 1983) is
the best book I have found on hope in the nuclear age, hope in
the face of the dragons of militarism, poverty, racism, sexism. Her
central image is of the woman in the Book of Revelation about
to give birth in the face of the dragon (Rev. 12). It is obvious that
once the baby is born, it will be devoured by the dragon. But
the woman finds the courage to believe that somehow life will
prevail. She dares to give birth to a tiny, fragile life.

Through Denise's words, I was challenged by both the woman
and Jesus to dare to believe as they did. I was being asked then
as I am being asked again now and am asking you — do we dare
to believe that if we set out with Jesus on the road of discipleship
and risk, losing our lives in the process, that somehow life will
prevail, that we will find that "fullness of life" that Jesus promises? If we sacrifice our lives daily through little acts of service,
as well as in larger ways, will it be worth it? Most people we
know cling to their lives and refuse to risk even in little ways,
much less risk it all. Are we crazy — or what?

I think we both have a sense that this road of discipleship
will involve risks, that it will mean losing our lives in at least
little ways, if not completely. The passage I cited above from the
U.S. Catholic bishops goes on to say: "To be a Christian ... is not
simply to believe with one's mind, but also to become a doer of
the word, a wayfarer with and a witness to Jesus. This means, of
course, that we never expect complete success within history and
that we must regard as normal even the path of persecution and
the possibility of martyrdom" (no. 276). That does not make me
comfortable at all! Even if we don't face martyrdom in a literal
sense, we sense at least its figurative possibilities. If we embrace
this call to be a disciple or prophet in our world, will we be able
to handle emotionally all the suffering people we will come to
know? What if a jobless or homeless person we befriend knocks
on our door and asks for more of our time and energy? What if
our spouse, partner, children, parents, friends, co-workers, boss

do not understand or even oppose us as we embrace this journey more seriously? Perhaps they already think we're crazy. Some disciples and prophets end up in jail. And some are even killed. Will any of that ever be asked of us? Where is all of this leading? Should we continue to work together to understand the meaning of discipleship? Do we dare to believe?

Believe in what? Do we dare believe that it is not hopeless, that despite the enormity of the problems confronting the world today, we can make a difference? Do we dare believe that Jesus is Lord of history and can take our tiny, fragile creative acts of love and resistance and combine them with those of millions of other disciples and prophets and realize in some way that Kingdom of Shalom promised by God through the Hebrew prophets? Do we choose the hope of the woman in the face of the dragon or do we choose to despair and do nothing other than "make the best of it for ourselves and family"? Do we believe that love and life are stronger than death, that truth will prevail over lies, that Jesus lives and we will too if we are willing to lose our lives in following him?

Believe in whom? Do I believe in a God who speaks to us in the same way God spoke to Jeremiah, intimately, tenderly? A song that runs through my mind and soul frequently has a comforting refrain: "Before the sun burned bright and rivers flowed, I called you each by name to share my home. No longer be afraid, you are my own. My love will never end. Halleluyah." I sing it often to remind myself of God's intimate love of me: "See! I will not forget you....I have carved you on the palm of my hand" (Isa. 49:15). God as potter and ourselves as clay molded lovingly is another special image of God for me (Jer. 18). John's Gospel describes us as branches attached to Jesus as the vine, with God as the loving vinedresser or pruner in our lives (John 15:1–7).

Psalm 139 is among the most consoling expressions of God's intimate love for us: "It was you who created my inmost self, and put me together in my mother's womb; for all these mysteries I thank you; for the wonder of myself, for the wonder of your works. You know me through and through, from having watched my bones take shape when I was being formed in secret, knitted together in the limbo of the womb" (Ps. 139:11–15).

This was the God that Jeremiah knew. Thus, he could hear and believe God's words to him: "Go now to those to whom I

send you and say whatever I command you. Do not be afraid
of them, for I am with you to protect you — it is Adonai who
speaks!" Can we hear and believe these words to us, as Jeremiah
did? Our God wants to send us forth again, perhaps this time
to people or places different than before. Are we ready to hear
where and to whom? Our God has something for us to say on
behalf of the Kingdom of Shalom. Are we ready to hear it? Are
we ready to accept ourselves as God accepts us — as persons
who have often deserted Jesus but who have been forgiven and
given his peace and Holy Spirit? We are loved and forgiven. And
because of this, we can love, forgive, and risk for others.

Are you ready to "go"? If you are like me, the answer is probably yes and no. If so, listen to these words from a contemporary
version of Jeremiah 1 and Isaiah 6:

THE LORD SAID, "GO"

And the Lord said, "Go!"
and I said, "Who, me?"
and God said, "Yes, you!"
and I said, "But I'm not ready yet,
and there is company coming,
and I can't leave my kids;
you know there's no one to take my place."
And God said, "You're stalling."

Again the Lord said, "Go!"
and I said, "But I don't want to,"
and God said, "I didn't ask if you wanted to."
And I said, "Listen, I'm not the kind of person
to get involved in controversy.
Besides, my family won't like it,
and what will the neighbors think!"
And God said, "Baloney!"

And yet a third time the Lord said, "Go!"
and I said, "Do I have to?"
and God said, "Do you love me?"
and I said, "Look, I'm scared....
People are going to hate me
and cut me up into little pieces.

I can't take it all by myself."
And God said, "Where do you think I'll be?"

And the Lord said, "Go!"
and I sighed,
"Here I am, send me!"[3]

For Reflection

1. Places where Jesus tells us what it means to follow him include the whole tenth chapter of Matthew's Gospel, Mark 8:34–38, and John 15:18–16:4.

2. Jesus makes it clear that even family members might not understand some of the steps along our journey and that we must be prepared for that rejection, but that the reward is infinitely better, including new "brothers and sisters" by the hundreds (Matt. 19:27–30 and Mark 10:28–31).

3. What are the fears or other obstacles that have kept you from setting out on the road of discipleship more boldly?

4. Is there anything you can do about those fears? We will come back to our fears in later chapters.

5. Do you ever feel hopeless? What about? Have you ever felt like the woman in the Book of Revelation, about to give birth in the face of the dragon? What did you decide to do?

6. Some dragons can seem overwhelming. When you hear that one child dies of starvation every two seconds (more than 40,000 every day) or, as one church document puts it, that this is a "moment of supreme crisis" because for the first time in history the human species has the power to destroy creation, how do you feel? What do you do and why?

7. Go back over your life and identify all those experiences that helped make you a more aware or concerned person — people you met, experiences you had, books you read. Write these down, perhaps in a journal. Then reflect on these experiences as "moments of movement," moments when God was leading you along your journey. Become as aware as you can of God's personal intervention in your life through so many different people and experiences and conclude your mental journey with a prayer of thanksgiving, perhaps the whole of Psalm 139.

Another way of concluding such a review is through song. One I like to sing reflectively is the St. Louis Jesuits' hymn, "Be

Not Afraid." The refrain and first verse are a good conclusion to
this step in our journey together:

> Be not afraid; I go before you always.
> Come, follow me, and I will give you rest.
>
> You shall cross the barren desert,
> but you shall not die of thirst.
> You shall wander far in safety,
> though you do not know the way.
> You shall speak your words in foreign lands
> and all will understand.
> Know that I am with you through it all.

Chapter 2

A Dream for the Journey

A JOURNEY IMPLIES A DESTINATION. The clearer or closer the destination, the more confidently and energetically we embrace the journey. If that journey involves risk, we are not likely to set out unless we have a clear sense of where we are headed and that the journey is worth the risk. Courageous, hopeful, faithful people — pilgrims, as they are often called — are people with a vision, a dream. They can set out on a journey across barren deserts and through raging waters, not even knowing the way, as long as there is a sense, a glimpse, of a final destination that is worth all the thirsting, risks, and uncertainties of the journey. The Hebrew patriarch Abraham and Sarah, his wife, were such persons; so was Dr. Martin Luther King, Jr. And so are we, if we are to become more courageous, compassionate, hopeful, faithful peacemakers, prophets, disciples of Jesus.

We too must see visions and dream dreams. We make a retreat or read a book like this in order to rekindle our dream. "Rekindle" is the right word, for we already have a dream. We would not be working through this book together if we didn't. But if you are like me, that dream needs to be rekindled periodically, so that we burn more passionately and compassionately inside and so our light shines more brightly outside. As we begin this chapter together, let's pray for God's Spirit of love to inspire and inflame our mind and heart: "Come, Holy Spirit, fill the hearts of your faithful and enkindle in us the fire of your love. Send forth your Spirit, Lord, and we will be re-created, and you will renew the face of the earth." Let's savor those words: *fill our hearts; enkindle in them the fire of your love; re-create us so that we can help transform the face of your earth. Yes, Lord!*

What impelled or empowered Abraham and Sarah to leave the security of their land and people and set out into the unknown? I think it must have been their conviction that they were called by a personal God who loved them deeply, that this "promised land" was far better than anything they had ever experienced, and that they could believe in this promise because it was made by a God who had always been faithful in keeping promises. Because Abraham and Sarah set out not knowing where they were going, St. Paul proclaimed them both as heroes of faith: "They died in faith, before receiving any of the things that had been promised, but they saw them in the far distance and welcomed them, recognizing that they were only strangers and nomads on earth" (Heb. 11:8–16).

The Biblical Dream

This "promised land" that they glimpsed from afar became clearer through the Hebrew prophets. God's Kingdom of Shalom became the Hebrew people's dream. As described in the Book of Isaiah:

> For now I create new heavens and a new earth, and the past will not be remembered.... Be glad and rejoice for ever and ever for what I am creating, because I now create Jerusalem "Joy" and her people "Gladness."... No more will the sound of weeping or the sound of cries be heard in her; in her no more will be found the infant living a few days only, or the old man not living to the end of his days.... They will build houses and inhabit them, plant vineyards and eat their fruit.... For my people shall live as long as trees, and my chosen ones wear out what their hands have made. They will not toil in vain or beget children to their own ruin, for they will be a race blessed by Adonai, and their children with them. Long before they call I shall answer; before they stop speaking I shall have heard. The wolf and the young lamb will feed together, the lion eat straw like the ox.... (Isa. 65:17–25)

To this and other prophetic descriptions of God's Kingdom of Shalom, Jesus added many parables as well as literal descriptions. The statement that sums it all up for me is that line from Jesus' "Last Discourse" in John's Gospel: "That they all may be one. Father, may they be one in us, as you are in me and I am in you... may they be one as we are one" (John 17:21–23). The oneness of all peoples, of all creation — this is God's Kingdom of Shalom. Paul writes of this vision as God's great mystery, or plan, for the world. "God has let us know the mystery of his purpose, the hidden plan he so kindly made in Christ from the beginning... that he would bring everything together under Christ, as head, everything in the heavens and everything on earth" (Eph. 1:9–10). Other translations speak of the reunification or reconciliation of all things in Christ.

Paul's whole letter to the Ephesians is a beautiful unveiling of this vision of reconciliation for the whole of creation. Paul starts with reconciliation at the level of husband and wife, urging both to love each other as much as Christ loved us all. Next, children and parents are to be reconciled. Third, members of local church communities need to see their different gifts as a source of enrichment and harmony, not a source of jealousy and division. On a societal or global scale, reconciliation calls for resisting the policies and values of the powers and the principalities that keep us at enmity with one another as whole peoples. Thus, our efforts at doing away with the clenched fist and the wicked word, as Isaiah writes (58:9), whether with our spouse, friend, children, co-workers, are as significant in God's plan as they are imperative. On a global scale, all that we do, for instance, to build bridges between ourselves as North Americans and the people and leaders of the Soviet Union, is of tremendous significance. We are participating in God's great mystery or plan for the world.

Finally, this mystery and ministry of reconciliation need to be extended to the earth itself. A compelling expression of this call comes from the pen of Chief Sealth (or Seattle) in his answer to a 1854 request from the U.S. government to buy his people's land near Seattle. In part he wrote:

> You must teach your children that the ground beneath their feet is the ashes of our grandfathers. So that they will respect the land, tell your children that the earth is rich with the lives of our kin. Teach your children what we have taught our children — that the earth is our mother. Whatever befalls the earth befalls the children of the earth. If you spit upon the ground, you spit upon yourselves. This we know. The earth does not belong to us; we belong to the earth. This we know. All things are connected like the blood which unites one family. All things are connected. Whatever befalls the earth befalls the children of the earth. We did not weave the

web of life; we are merely strands in it. Whatever we do to the web, we do to ourselves. So love the earth as we have loved it. Care for it as we have cared for it. And with all your heart, with all your mind, with all your spirit, love it as God loves us all.

Our Place in the Dream

Our Jewish/Christian vision of Shalom is of the oneness of the human family at one with the earth itself. This vision for the whole of creation has profound implications for our role as agents of God's reconciliation of all in Christ. Who are we in all of this? What has God called us to be and how are we to think of ourselves now? There are many images in the Christian Scriptures that should help rekindle our vision and mobilize our will. Let's consider five: light, salt, friend, new creation, and ambassadors of reconciliation.

Light

In Matthew 5:13–16, Jesus says we are to be a "light for the world," so that the world may see the good that we do and give glory to God. We are to "shine before all," to be placed on a mountain top for all to see. But we are tempted in two quite different ways to deny this reality of who we are. The first is to want to remain hidden, not quite so noticeable in our peace-making work. I don't want the IRS to come after our family or Institute, for instance, so I am tempted to compromise my opposition to paying for war. Have you ever found yourself not wanting to jeopardize your reputation, job, your other projects by being too public?

The second temptation is to call attention to ourselves, to focus praise on ourselves rather than on the God whose grace is the source of our power — "for the Kingdom, the power and the glory are yours...." Light enables others to be seen. Our light should enable the Word of God, in Scripture and in the person of Jesus, to be more readily seen. If we preach, we are to preach Christ, not ourselves.

Salt

"Salt of the earth," Jesus calls us. "If the salt loses its flavor, it is good for nothing." We all experience times when we feel "tasteless," when we feel we are "going on old notes." The first temptation is to settle for this mediocrity — accepting the relatively nonthreatening niche that a society grants its "radicals" if they don't challenge it too fundamentally. When we experience either the tastelessness of our "old notes" or the comfortableness of our position in society, we are challenged to break out of these "old wine skins."

The second temptation for salt is similar to that of light — to call attention to itself. The function of salt is not primarily to be tasty itself but to bring out the flavor in others. Persons who love to salt their ear of corn, for instance, never lick their lips over how delicious the salt tastes. Rather, they proclaim the wonders of the corn. In our work with the so-called powerless or voiceless peoples of our communities, nation, and world, we are to enter into a partnership with them: "Never be condescending but make real friends with the poor" (Rom. 12:16). We are to be a "voice with" even more than a "voice for" the voiceless victims of injustice. Better still, we are called to empower them to find and use their own voices and not remain "voiceless victims." That takes humility, listening, a breaking down of stereotypes. Gandhi sent his "satyagrahis" (his followers of nonviolence), especially the middle- or upper-class urban ones, into the villages to work side by side with the poor, to lose their exalted images of themselves as India's future leaders, to discover the potential and virtues of the poor, and then to mobilize that potential.

Chosen Friends

Jesus chose us, not vice versa. He wants us as friends, not servants. What does it mean to be a "friend"? We talk freely with a good friend. We take "quality time" for a good friend. We walk in silence with a good friend. We are willing to sacrifice greatly for a good friend, perhaps even to the point of laying down our life: "Greater love than this no one has than to lay down their life for their friend" (John 15:13–16). Jesus is that kind of friend, our "good shepherd" who literally laid down his life for his sheep whom he knew as intimately as friends (John 10:6–18). Near the end of his life Gandhi prepared himself and his closest satyagrahis to go singly into the villages where Hindu-Muslim violence was at its peak. According to Pyarelal, his secretary, he said, "I can go alone into all this violence as a nonviolent presence

because I know that Jesus walks with me." Gandhi nurtured that
personal friendship by daily prayer. There has to be time in our
busy lives for the openness and communication that can enable
us to experience and deepen our reality as "friends" of Jesus.

A New Creation

Like St. Paul, we are challenged to be able to say more fully
each day that it is "no longer I who live but Christ who lives
in me..." (Gal. 2:20). "For anyone who is in Christ, there is a
new creation" (2 Cor. 5:17). Thomas Merton in his *New Seeds of
Contemplation* writes about our "true self" and our "false self."
Our true self he describes as an "echo of God" — a reflection of
God's love in and for the world, sharing in God's voice, God's
light.

Even more compelling to me is the image of a new creation
provided by Etty Hillesum in her inspiring diary *An Interrupted
Life*. This rescuer of Jews during World War II and a victim herself
of Hitler's extermination camps speaks of the followers of Jesus as
"melodies of God." She writes: "Melodious rolls the world from
God's right hand. I too wanted to roll melodiously out of God's
hand." I like Mary Lou Kownacki's commentary on this passage
as much as the passage itself: "We call these melodies of God the
pure of heart. In a sense they are always in a posture of worship,
of adoration, of thanksgiving. Just as the beatitude promises,
the pure of heart do see God. They see God everywhere and in
everyone. Consequently the only possible posture for the grateful
is resistance. Always those in awe of the gift of life must resist
the manufacture of death."[4]

When I think about being a "melody of God," I think immediately of Francis of Assisi, Jesus' troubadour singing and dancing
through central Italy. We are to become "joyful echoes" of God's
voice. The temptation here is to fail to nurture that joyfulness
that attracts others far more than our heavy political analyses,
unintentional guilt trips, or bitter diatribes. (Overwork and burn
out are often the result when we forget that we are friends of the
Messiah, not the Messiah himself.)

Ambassadors of Reconciliation

As joyful echoes of God, we can be ambassadors of Christ,
ambassadors of reconciliation, as Paul describes us in his letter

to the Corinthians: "It was God who reconciled us to himself through Christ and gave us the work of handing on this reconciliation. . . . So we are ambassadors of Christ; it is as though God were appealing through us . . . : be reconciled to God. For our sake God made the sinless one into sin, so that in him we might become the goodness of God" (2 Cor. 5:18–21).

Despite what others call us, we are not "ambassadors of the Soviet Union," but neither are we "ambassadors of the United States" (or Canada or . . .). We are ambassadors of Christ, ambassadors of reconciliation, ambassadors of truth. We are to bear witness to the truth, Jesus says. And this truth is that we are all one, that God has reconciled all peoples in Christ, and that we are to live as one, as brother and sister, and that the true test of our oneness is whether we love our enemies and are willing to love to the point of laying down our lives for others. This is what reconciliation means, for Jesus died for all. It is by the blood of Christ that all barriers are broken down, hostility melted, divisions overcome (Eph. 2:13–16).

Calling Us to Hope

With such a vision, both of creation as a whole and our role within it, how can we not be on fire all the time? Why are we so often more tasteless than salty? Why is our light at times so dim? Why do we experience ourselves as reluctant pilgrims at best, often unwilling to embrace the uncertainties along the road of discipleship? I can speak only for myself in trying to answer these questions.

Allan Boesak

On a societal level, my experience is probably similar to yours. I see so much violence and injustice in the world, so many signs of the "non-Shalom," as it were, that it is hard at times to really believe in God's promise. Allan Boesak's wrestling with the injustice of apartheid challenges my sense of hope and causes me to dig more deeply than ever before for the source of my hope for the coming of the Kingdom of Shalom. Coming from Allan, one of the most prophetic and persecuted Black Christian leaders in South Africa, this reflection is coming from the heart of a passionate believer. It has a little bit of Job's struggle in it. In fact, you might go back and read Job's laments over the injustice he experienced in the world around him (Job 24:2–3 and 9–12; 30:21–27). Allan entitles his reflection "The Presence of the Living God," and in it he describes his experience of standing with the Black residents of a little village in South Africa, anticipating that government bulldozers will destroy their homes at any minute. He prayed and sang with them all night and listened to the stories of how they came to Mogopa seventy years ago and made it their home. Then he asked himself and us:

At this I had to ask myself, what are we doing here? Where is this God of love and justice and mercy we were telling the Mogopa people about? As I saw them breaking down their own homes ("before the government does it"), I was overcome with a deep despair. Isn't there anything else we can do besides pray and assure these people that God is just, that God is love and is on their side, that God will not forget them?

A journalist confronted me and put the same question to me. Is this not, he asked, a perfect example of religion being the opiate of the people? I had to think about that.

And then I knew. Sometimes the church can do nothing but pray with the people, become one with them in their silent suffering. The church must assure them that God is not aloof, but present in the situation, in their pain, sharing their despair and suffering.

But God's presence is not a placating presence, it is a protesting and comforting presence. God is with them not to bless the lie that is happening to them, but to remind them of the truth that is being crushed to earth but that shall rise again. It is not a presence that says, "be still," but a presence that says, "don't accept it." God's presence reminds us that such oppression, greed, and mindless inhumanity are not of God. These are lies that must be overcome by the truth that God reveals.

It is the truth that Jesus Christ alone is Lord, that he is our life and the life of the world. It is the truth that God is not honored or glorified by illness, poverty, dejection, or exploitation. God is not honored by death and destruction, by the inhumanity of apartheid. God is not honored by the untimely death of little children who suffer hunger while the tables of the rich are sagging under the weight of surplus food.

God is not honored by the naked cynicism of those who seek peace through the terror of the nuclear threat. These are the lies that God's presence in suffering unmasks. And at the same time this presence reveals the truth, and we must shout it from the roof tops.[5]

Are we prepared to "shout it from the roof tops" that apartheid, hunger, exploitation, are not God's will, as Allan has become willing to do, at the risk of his own life and that of his wife and children? Yes and no is the best I can answer at this point in my life. I wish my voice were bolder, that I wouldn't shy away from roof tops as much as I do. But I'm not sure what would happen to me if I were bolder. I think this is what keeps me from being the prophet and disciple Jesus wants. My societal-level doubts about the reality of God's promise of a Kingdom of Shalom get mixed up with my personal-level brokenness.

What is this personal-level brokenness? The need to be in control, to be secure, to call the shots. I find it hard to "let go and let God" lead, as the experience of Alcoholics Anonymous puts it. I'm much more comfortable being in the driver's seat in our car, literally. It is a good analogy for my whole relationship with God. I think I can say that I am not as control-oriented as I used to be. I have taken some small leaps of faith into the uncertainties of discipleship and have occasionally relinquished the driver's seat. One of the most appealing images given to me in the midst of a personal crisis two years ago was that of Jesus and me on a bicycle built for two. Jesus had the handle bars in front and I was on the second seat. Every time I stopped pedaling out of depression, despair, or fatigue, he would say, "Just keep pedaling, Jim, and don't worry; I'll do the steering." I still feel more comfortable when I'm in control (of my work, my children, other relationships). I still want some of the world's security. But I'm getting better at pedaling from the second seat.

Martin Luther King

One who has helped me deal with the temptation to give up on my dream and settle for something more comfortable and secure is Martin Luther King, Jr. I have a video on Dr. King entitled *Trumpet of Conscience* that I use in all my retreats. The final segment of this celebration of Dr. King's prophetic witness is his Christmas 1967 sermon at Ebenezer Baptist Church in Atlanta, where he acknowledged his struggle to keep his dream alive:

> If there is to be peace on earth and goodwill to all, we must finally believe in the ultimate morality of the universe and believe that all reality hinges on moral foundations. Truth crushed to earth will rise again. No lie can live forever. I tried to talk to the nation about a dream that I had. And I must confess to you today that not long after talking about that dream, I started seeing it turn into a nightmare. Yes, I'm personally the victim of deferred dreams, of blasted hopes. In spite of that, I close today by saying, I still have a dream. Because, you know, you can't give up in life. If you lose hope, somehow you lose that vitality that keeps life moving. You lose that courage to be, that quality that helps you go on in spite of. And so this is our faith. As we continue to hope for peace on earth and goodwill to all, let us know that in the process we have cosmic companionship.
>
> And so today I still have a dream. People will rise up and come to see that they are made to live together as brothers and sisters. I still have a dream today that one day every person of color in the world will be judged on the content of their character rather than the color of their skin; and everyone will respect the dignity and worth of human personality; and brotherhood will be more than a few words at the end of a prayer, but the first order of business on every legislative agenda. I still have a dream today. Justice will roll down like waters and righteousness like a mighty stream. I still have a dream today — that war will come to an end, that individuals will beat their swords into plowshares and their spears into pruning hooks, and nations will no longer rise up against nations. Neither will they study war anymore. I still have a dream.

Let's pause for a moment and thank God for the Etty Hillesums, Allan Boesaks, and Martin Luther Kings of our era, for their willingness to embrace the risks of discipleship and show us that such courage, love, hope, and fidelity are possible in our time.

For Reflection

1. Besides returning to the Isaiah 65:17–25 passage, you might pray over the following prophetic descriptions of God's Kingdom of Shalom: Isaiah 2:4 and 32:15–20; Amos 9:13–15; and Ezekiel 34:23–31, where the prophet describes Adonai's "covenant of Shalom."

2. How does your vision or dream compare with the one developed throughout this chapter?

3. When you think about Shalom as the reunification or reconciliation of all things in Christ, what in your life takes on special significance? Does this excite you or rekindle your fire, at least a little?

4. In what ways can you envision yourself as an "echo" or "melody" of God? How to deepen this realization and find additional ways of living it out is the task of this book.

5. Go back to Job's struggle and Allan Boesak's questions about social injustice: Where do we and the people of Mogopa find hope? For what do I pray? In what do I believe?

6. What keeps Allan Boesak going? What enabled Martin Luther King to still have a dream, despite its continual frustration? What can we do to keep our dream alive?

Our journey will take us through many more barren deserts and raging waters, but we need not be afraid, for God promises to be with us through it all. God's Spirit of Love is a powerful provision to have in our backpack!

Chapter 3

The Power of Suffering Love

IF YOU FELT A LITTLE ANXIETY OR FEAR in chapter 1 around the reflection on the cost of discipleship, it was well founded. This chapter focuses directly on the cost of discipleship, the price of peacemaking. The dream we considered in the last chapter would be incomplete without examining how peacemaking, Shalom, or reconciliation is brought about. As Paul tells us in Ephesians, it is by the blood of Christ that reconciliation is accomplished: "But now in Christ Jesus you who once were far off have been brought near in the blood of Christ. For he is our peace, who has made us both one, and has broken down the dividing wall of hostility...so making peace, and might reconcile us both to God in one body through the cross, thereby bringing the hostility to an end" (Eph. 2:13–16). The price of peace isn't cheap. It will cost us our lives, just as it cost Jesus his.

The price of peacemaking is the same as the power of the peacemaker. It is the power of suffering love, as Gandhi put it:

Up to the year 1906 [in South Africa], I simply relied on appeal to reason....Since then the conviction has been growing upon me that things of fundamental importance to the people are not secured by reason alone but have to be purchased with their suffering. Suffering is the law of human beings; war is the law of the jungle. But suffering is infinitely more powerful than the law of the jungle for converting the opponent and opening his ears, which are otherwise shut, to the voice of reason. Nobody has probably drawn up more petitions or espoused more forlorn causes than I and I have come to this fundamental conclusion that if you want something really important to be done, you must not merely satisfy the reason, you must move the heart also. The appeal of reason is more to the head but the penetration of the heart comes from suffering. It opens up the inner understanding in people. Suffering is the badge of the human race, not the sword.[6]

This is the power of nonviolent love. We meet it throughout the Scriptures. In Isaiah, the Messiah is described as the "suffering servant." "He will bring true justice to the nations...[but] he does not break the bruised reed or snuff out the smoldering wick" (Isa. 42:1–4). "I offered my back to those who struck me, my cheeks to those who tore at my beard," he says of himself (Isa. 50:4–11). "On him lies a punishment that brings us peace, and through his wounds we are healed.... Harshly dealt with, he bore it humbly; he never opened his mouth, like a lamb that is led to the slaughter-house.... If he offers his life in atonement, he shall see his heirs, he shall have a long life and through him what Adonai wishes will be done" (Isa. 52:13–53:12).

Jesus takes up the mantle of the suffering servant and becomes the "lamb of God who takes away the sin of the world" and reconciles us with God and with one another. Paul continues this reflection in his letters. "Resist evil and conquer it with good" (Rom. 12:21). The "good" that Paul describes in this section of Romans includes "blessing those who persecute us," "equal kindness," offering food to our enemies if they are hungry or drink if they are thirsty. In reaching out to our so-called enemies as persons, we distinguish the persons from the actions or policies needing resistance.

Paul is paralleled by Matthew 5:38–48, where love of enemies and resisting injustice are described in terms of turning the other cheek, walking the extra mile, and giving the undergarment as well as the coat. These "transforming initiatives," as some have called them,[7] transform a situation of injustice and conflict by startling the oppressor and public opinion into a new way of seeing the victims and their victimization. This is Gandhi's path of suffering love as well as Jesus' way in embracing his cross. It is this kind of love that Martin Luther King preached and lived. Let's listen to his words:

There is another word for love. It is agape. Agape is more than romantic love. It is more than friendship. Agape is understanding, creative, redemptive good-will for all. Agape is an overflowing love, expecting nothing in return. Theologians describe it as the love of God operating in the human heart. And so when you rise to love at this level, you love all persons not because you like them, not because their ways appeal to you, but you love every person because God loves them. This is what Jesus meant when He said, "love your enemies." And I'm happy He didn't say "like your enemies" because there are people I find it pretty difficult to like. Like is an affectionate emotion and I can't like anybody bombing my home. I can't like anybody who would exploit me. I can't like anybody who would trample over me with injustice. I can't like anybody who threatens to kill me day in and day out.

Jesus reminds us that love is greater than like. Love is understanding, creative, redemptive good-will for all persons. I've seen too much hate to want to hate myself. Hate is too great a burden to bear. Somehow we must be able to stand up before our most embittered opponents and say we will match your capacity to inflict suffering with our capacity to endure suffering. We will meet your physical force with soul force. Do to us what you will and we will still love you. Throw us in jail and we will still love you. Send your hooded perpetrators of violence into our communities after the midnight hour and drag us out on some wayside road and leave us half-dead as you beat us and we will still love you. But be you assured that we will wear you down by our capacity to suffer. And we will so appeal to your heart and conscience that we will win you in the process. And our victory will be a double victory.[8]

Such love would be unbelievable if we didn't have those images before us of Dr. King and his followers, children and adults, spit at, clubbed, attacked by police dogs, cannonaded with fire hoses, thrown into paddy wagons and jailed, shot. We have the image of Jesus on a cross before us frequently, but how often have we really looked at that image and taken it in? That's the kind of Lord we are to follow? That much love? Be a "lamb"?

As the message and witness of Jesus, Gandhi, King, and so many others have shown, the answer to "how far are we to go?" is "all the way." Daily and ultimately, figuratively and literally, we are asked to lay down our lives for others. The words and emotion of two Nicaraguan mothers who had recently lost their sons in the struggle against the Contras seared their way into my heart as I listened to them in the northern city of Jalapa right after Christmas in 1983: "This is how we can live out the words of Jesus, to lay down our lives for others and then forgive those who killed our sons." My eyes were riveted on their faces and I could see the depth of love and forgiveness behind their words.

Personal Implications

Reconciliation

The dying to ourselves involved in such a life of reconciliation and nonviolence is a daily challenge. It can begin with the tiny struggles to love those with whom we are at odds in some way. For me, this is frequently our teenaged children. Sometimes I feel the desire to retaliate, to get even, when I feel wronged by them. "That's the last favor I'll do for you for a long time, buster!" has come to my lips more than once. This is my opportunity to learn the power of suffering or agapaic love.

Several years ago I was given a stick of salami during Holy Week while I was fasting, so I put it in the back of the refrigerator to save for after Easter. To appreciate the import of this story, you need to know how much I love salami! But on Easter Monday I discovered that others had found the salami and only a tiny bit remained. I was furious and let it be known that the culprits would have to buy me another one, immediately. I stormed around the house shouting my anger at this inconsiderateness, blasting the kids verbally. This wasn't the first time something like this had happened. I had to put a stop to it now. But how? I had blasted the kids verbally before and it hadn't worked. Why not try a different tactic? So more for strategic than virtuous reasons, I tried one of those "transforming initiatives" like turning the other cheek. I went out and bought another salami myself and had a surprise "happy hour" before dinner in which the whole family could enjoy the salami. I'm not sure about the impact of that initiative on the kids, but it did transform my heart a little and has led me to look for similar approaches in other confrontational situations. The capacity to forgive is absolutely essential to love, especially to loving our enemies, as Dr. King points out so well: "Forgiveness is a catalyst creating the atmosphere necessary for a fresh start and a new beginning. . . . The evil deed [of an enemy] is no longer a mental block impeding a new relationship."[9]

Nonviolence involves confrontation, yes, but confrontation whose goal is reconciliation. Dr. King certainly did not avoid confrontation. His *Letter from a Birmingham City Jail* is a moving response to his critics who challenged his commitment to nonviolence because his tactics regularly provoked violence. In his reply, Dr. King distinguished a "positive peace" from a "negative peace," which he equated with keeping the lid on violent situations and pretending that this so-called order was the same as peace. The negative peace of injustice or "institutional violence" has to be brought to the light of day so that it can be transformed into a "positive peace," a peace that encompasses justice and love (Shalom). How we surface an issue, how we confront those who we think have wronged us is the key, whether they be family members, friends, co-workers, government officials.

Jesus provides guidance for us in his teaching on correcting our brothers or sisters (Matt. 18:15–18). The first step is not to call a press conference and denounce the person in public, but to try ways of converting the person in private. Gandhi gives us examples of how to do this at all levels. One of the keys to his approach was truthfulness. We must always recognize that "our truth" is not "the truth" and that our opponents may well have a piece of the truth as well. We have to be committed to "the truth" above all, which means clinging to what we believe is our portion of the truth ("satyagraha" means "clinging to the truth") while remaining open to our opponents' portion of the truth. This requires honest searching, a willingness to acknowledge our brokenness and portion of the blame for the conflict, humility, courage, and a willingness to "die" to ourselves.

"Experiments with Truth"

All this we can practice daily. I think of this practicing as a series of what Gandhi calls "experiments with truth." He became the person we know today by just such a life of experimenting with the truth. He was not always the great person we read about and admire. He *became* Gandhi, precisely by working at it daily. We can experiment with the truth of suffering love daily as well. Refusing to think the worst of my children when they make mistakes, continuing to love them through the messiness and pain of adolescence, continuing to do "favors" even when I have to confront them about their negative behavior — I am really having to work at this. In the midst of a family member's failures, we can choose to let our negative feelings dominate or we can refuse to think the worst and choose to think the best about that person. "Worst case scenarios" may be common to military planners, but they must not prevail for people who want to practice nonviolence or suffering love.

How many times could we take the first step toward reconciliation with someone with whom we are at odds, especially when we think they are at fault and should come to us? Swallowing our pride, as it were, and offering reconciling gestures does not have to mean allowing ourselves to be walked on. That's important especially for women. There's a difference between suffering love and taking abuse from someone whose behavior needs to be challenged.[10*] The "suffering servant" passages in Isaiah need to be read with this realization. Jesus was a "lamb" and so are we to become, but Jesus also says to us: "Remember, I am sending you out like sheep among wolves; so be cunning as serpents and yet as harmless as doves" (Matt. 10:16).

This "cunning" for me means primarily thinking through conflict situations carefully and identifying strategies that will have a chance of promoting reconciliation. One of the most helpful resources for me along this line has been a book by a friend named Dudley Weeks, entitled *Conflict Partnership*. Dudley's thought and practice have been greatly influenced by both Gandhi and King. His approach is similar — view our conflicts as something between ourselves and our opponents that is keeping us apart, something both of us need to address as "partners" against this barrier between us, and work with our opponents in such a way that they begin to see the conflict in these same terms. In my case, it might sound like — "Son, there's something going on between us that isn't good. I'd really like to figure out with you what it is, so that we can work to change it. I want us to enjoy each other more, rather than always be fighting." Dudley offers a wealth of practical strategies for approaching conflicts this way and for bringing our opponents around to this same way of viewing conflicts.[11*]

Another area in which we can be conducting experiments with the truth of suffering love is our willingness to sacrifice for others. Jesus, Gandhi, King, and the two Nicaraguan mothers did not willingly sacrifice their own lives or their sons' without many prior tiny sacrifices. There were countless ways Jesus learned to sacrifice himself as he was growing up in a poor home in a poor land. In his public ministry, he learned daily what "availability to others" meant. He learned in his desert retreats, in his fasting and other forms of self-denial, in his patient nurturing of his disciples, most of whom eventually deserted him. More and more courageously Jesus conformed his will to the demanding mission given him by God.

Gandhi and "Ahimsa" " Non violent love "

Gandhi's experiments with truth took him along a similar journey. He realized early on that the root of violence is a desire to put "me first." Humans violate or exploit one another and the earth because of a desire to enrich ourselves. Personal greed is the source of violence. I must preserve and enrich myself at all costs. Often this "self" gets extended to include family, tribe, clan, community, nation — with poverty and war as the results. The way to root out this internal source of human violence is to begin at the personal level and our "me-ism." It is in this context that we have to understand Gandhi's many experiments with food and fasting, with sexuality and his eventual commitment to celibacy, with cleaning toilets and other menial tasks, with community living, with prayer and silence. Each area offered him dozens of ways he could, in the words of Jim Douglass, who probably knows Gandhi better than any North American today, "reduce himself to zero" and become a pure instrument of God's power of love and truth in the world.

In Jim's prophetic book *Lightning East to West*, he quotes Gandhi's secretary Pyarelal on Gandhi's understanding of the spiritual equivalent of Einstein's "$E = mc^2$," a power that could match, even surpass, the power of the atom in nuclear bombs: "The corresponding law governing the release of spiritual energy is to be found in the formula enunciated by Gandhi, viz. that even an infinitesimal of an individual, when he has realized the ideal of *Ahimsa* [nonviolent love] in its fullness so that in thought, word and deed, he — in short, his whole being — becomes a function of *Ahimsa* as it were, he becomes filled with its power, the power of love, soul force, truth force, or the godhead within us, to which there is no limit and before which all opposition and hatred must cease...."[12]

Fasting

Fasting was one of Gandhi's principal instruments in his struggle with himself, just as it was one of Jesus' means of learning to sacrifice himself. In fact, fasting is a special means of self-sacrifice in most religious traditions. There are many forms of fasting. Some persons cannot fast from food. They might consider other forms of fasting — from television, from cigarettes, from liquor, from talking, from whatever we overindulge in and that keeps us from being more single-minded about "seeking first the Kingdom of God." Recall the U.S. Catholic bishops' imperative that we "separate ourselves from all attachments and affiliation that could prevent us from hearing and following our authentic vocation."

I am hesitant to write about something as interior as fasting, especially when my own experiments with fasting from food and drink have not always gone well. I am very aware of my weaknesses that are both revealed and challenged when I fast. The Methodist bishops of the U.S. write in their prophetic 1986 document *In Defense of Creation* that "the disciplines of fasting and penance temper our passions, our indulgences, and our ambitions" (pp. 84–85). The Catholic bishops add in their document that fasting is "a tangible sign of our need and desire to do penance..., to make reparation for the violence in our own lives and in our world" (nos. 297–298).

The bishops also remind us of other ways of fasting as well as the spirit that must accompany our fasting, when they quote Isaiah 58:6–10:

> Is not this the sort of fast that pleases me, to break unjust fetters and undo the thongs of the yoke, to let the oppressed go free and break every yoke, to share your bread with the hungry and shelter the homeless poor, to clothe the person you see to be naked and not turn from your own kin? Then will your light shine like the dawn and your wound be quickly healed over. If you do away with the yoke, the clenched fist, the wicked word, if you give your bread to the hungry and relief to the oppressed, your light will rise in the darkness, and your shadows become like noon.

External fasting is not enough. God wants much more — to let go of myself and any behavior that might hurt or exploit others

and to rely totally on God. Fasting from food *can* help, but only
if done in the proper spirit. Am I more loving on my fast days?
Letting go of wicked words and clenched fists can be a more
pleasing and effective form of fasting. And there can be a lot of
self-denial involved in confronting the yokes of exploitation in
society as well as in sharing our food and clothing, and especially
in opening our hearts and homes to the homeless.

The call to fasting as a means of reparation for our violence
as individuals and collectively as a nation is striking a responsive
chord in many persons. The challenge that all our churches are
issuing to us believers, that we take greater risks for peace and
justice, demands that we become both prophetic and prayerful.
I believe that we will be truly prophetic over the long haul only
to the extent that we become more prayerful as we confront the
dragons of our time — the arms race, militarism and other forms
of violence, poverty, racism, sexism.

First, then, fasting is a call to prayer. Fast days should be
special days of prayer, of prayer not just in periods set aside
for reflection on the Scriptures but primarily in tiny moments
throughout the day. In fasting from food, there are often many
moments of wanting to eat. These moments become invitations
to prayer — to speak with Jesus, to be more fully aware of his
presence, to beg him for peace, to be reminded that God's will
for the world truly is Shalom. When our fast days are regular —
at least weekly — this sense of prayerfulness seems to carry over
to other days as well. Some people combine their fast days with
silence to focus more consciously on the presence of God in creation, in other people, and in their own hearts.

Second, fasting is a means of self-emptying. Central to a
prayerful spirit is the desire to empty ourselves so that we can
be filled with God's Spirit. This *kenosis*, or self-emptying, can
focus on more than food and drink. We can limit our agenda
of activities on our fast days, to give God an opportunity to fill
our schedule. As a person struggling with the desire to always
be in control, I know I benefit from lightening my work load on
fast days and being open to God's surprises (people, thoughts,
magazines, crises on the home front).

Third, fasting is a way of expressing our dependence on God.
The overwhelming sense of evil manifested in the arms race and
the other dragons of our time brings me to my knees, figuratively

and literally. This sense of evil can drive us on to work harder for peace and justice, but it should also drive us back to God. After we have done what we can — writing government leaders, giving talks, mobilizing local groups, setting up or participating in "urgent action networks," vigiling and demonstrating, resisting war taxes — we are faced with the realization that all that is still not enough. I find myself praying in such moments: "God, we depend on you. Raise up ever more courageous instruments of your peace, including myself. Work your miracles through others. Touch the hearts of decision makers. Give courage to those victimized by the evils we are resisting. Give us greater courage, hope, and insight into your will and our role."

Fourth, and related to self-emptying, fasting is an instrument of discipleship. Jesus challenges us in the Gospels about whether we have "counted the cost" of following him (see, for example, Luke 14:25–33). Are we really willing to suffer or are we just "hanging around" the Gospel, as it were? The tiny acts of self-denial involved in fasting can be a preparation for the greater demands of suffering love I anticipate God will make of us in the future. Laying down our lives generally proceeds one step at a time. Martyrdom comes rather far down the line! The pruning process (John 15:1–7) that God has in mind for each of us — calling us to be ever more willing to let go and follow Jesus — involves many moments of self-denial. Fasting can be an important part of this process of dying to ourselves, preparing us to lay down our lives more fully and freely along our journey.

Fifth, fasting is a means of solidarity. The tiny no of self-denial can also be a tiny yes of solidarity. We can experience many moments of solidarity on fast days, when we bring to mind the lives of those victimized by the evils we are resisting — for me, friends in Central America, other victims of injustice around the world, the people in the shelters and nursing homes I visit as a clown in St. Louis, friends who are hurting. I find it especially helpful to focus each fast day on a particular person or group. The struggle to say no to food and drink is easier when I have someone specific to offer up that sacrifice for, someone who helps motivate me to this tiny sacrifice. I find the inner bond with that person or people deepened by the fast day, and my willingness to sacrifice for them in other ways is increased. We make sacrifices for people we love. The deeper the bond, the more willing we generally are to give of ourselves. Fasting can strengthen that bond.

Last, fasting is an invitation to service. The section on fasting in the U.S. Catholic bishops' document includes the recommendation that fasting "be accompanied by works of charity and service toward our neighbors." Fast days are opportunities for fuller presence to those around us, if we do not allow our work schedule to dominate the day. Special little acts of service — doing an extra task for someone we live with, a phone call or letter to a hurting friend or relative, time for a co-worker at the office — make the solidarity of fasting more genuine. Those closest to us should also be the beneficiaries of our fasting.

For Reflection

1. Recall Isaiah's description of the suffering servant in 42:1–4 as one who "will not break a bruised reed or snuff out a smoldering wick." Just as God accepts our brokenness, we have many opportunities to see beyond the worst in others and nurture the best in them — family members, friends, co-workers. What are ways you can help build up the "bruised reeds" in your life?

2. Peter 3:8–9 instructs us not to return evil for evil or insult for insult, but to return a blessing instead. Are there situations where you could apply this teaching? How?

3. Psalm 19:10–11, 15 reflects on the importance of loving words. We all know how easily our tongues can wound others. What are ways you can practice "nonviolence of the tongue"?

4. Pray over the Isaiah passages on the suffering servant (42:1–4; 49:1–6; 50:4–11; 52:13–53:12), as well as the description of *agape* by Martin Luther King. Write down for yourself ways you can practice such love.

5. Do you need to pay more attention to the image of Jesus crucified? If so, you might consider wearing a cross as a pin or chain around your neck, putting it on prayerfully each day; or hang a crucifix at home or work where you will see it regularly.

6. Pick that member of the animal kingdom that you would most like to be, if you had to be animal. What are the characteristics of the an animal you chose? How do these compare with Jesus' choice of a "lamb"?

7. In the reflection about laying down our lives for others,

was there something that spoke to your present circumstances? Should you act? If so, you might find it helpful to make a plan.

8. What are the attachments in your life that keep you from being a more single-minded disciple of Jesus? Given your health, family, and work situations, what makes the most sense for you in terms of fasting or other ways of dealing with these attachments?

I realize that these are not easy questions and that there is much to reflect on here. So I conclude with advice I have to remind myself of often. Take one step at a time! In answering these eight questions myself, I could list a hundred things I should be doing that I'm not. That would overwhelm me, so instead I identify several possibilities, choose one to start with, and then come back to the others after I have gotten far enough along on the one to warrant moving on. Remember, "Gandhi became Gandhi" — by a series of experiments with truth, one step at a time. Because he remained faithful to such experimentation over an entire lifetime, he had time to take many steps in his journey.

Francis of Assisi offers a beautiful concluding prayer that expresses the essence of suffering love in simple terms for people like you and me who need to see such a challenging concept in "do-able" terms. Others have put this "peace prayer" to music. If you know it in musical form, sing it often. If you want a copy of it as a prayer card, write me.

> Lord, make me an instrument of Your peace;
> where there is hatred, let me sow love;
> where there is injury, pardon;
> where there is doubt, faith;
> where there is despair, hope;
> where there is darkness, light;
> and where there is sadness, joy.
> O Divine Master,
> grant that I may not so much seek
> to be consoled as to console;
> to be understood as to understand;
> to be loved as to love.
> For it is in giving that we receive;
> it is in pardoning that we are pardoned;
> and it is in dying that we are born to eternal life.

Chapter 4

Peacemaking and Prayer

GANDHI, KING, FRANCIS, Jim and Shelley Douglass, Mary Lou Kownacki, the two Nicaraguan mothers, and all the other courageous and compassionate peacemakers I know are people of prayer. How often Jesus withdrew from the press of people and tasks to be with his God and to connect with those people and tasks in a much deeper way. Jesus began his public ministry with a forty-day retreat in the wilderness and returned to the wilderness regularly. Why is prayer so essential for peacemaking?

Contemplative Prayer

Contemplation and Peacemaking

In "Contemplation and Ministry," Henri Nouwen describes how contemplation is integral to ministry.[13]* The vision that we share in our ministry is revealed to us in prayer. In order to "see" God in the people with whom we minister, to enable them to see God in themselves, and for all of us to see God in the creation around us, we need to withdraw in prayer. The reason Mother Teresa is able to say in all honesty that she sees God in the faces of the destitute and dying with whom she lives is her contemplative union with God in prayer. In these times of silent presence before God, we discover God dwelling within us ("Make your home in me as I make mine in you," Jesus says — John 15:4), and not only within us but within each person made in God's image and likeness and within all of creation.

Thomas Merton, another deeply prayerful peacemaker, dramatically describes the fruit of this contemplative understanding: "Then it was as if I suddenly saw the secret beauty of their hearts, the depths of their hearts where neither sin nor desire nor self knowledge can reach, the core of their reality, the person that each one is in God's eyes. If only they could see themselves as they really are. If only we could see each other that way all the time, there would be no more war, no more hatred, no more cruelty, no more greed.... I suppose the big problem would be that we would fall down and worship each other."[14*] How different our attitude, our words, our actions would be toward the people with whom we interact each day if we really sensed "that of God" in them, as the Quakers put it. How different our attitude and actions toward all the earth would be if we really sensed the Creator's hand and presence in everything. To do so, we need to withdraw from the press of people and tasks and be silent in places where we can sense God's presence.

The more we begin to see God's presence in all around us, the more our conviction grows that God is truly present and acting in the world. This is an aspect of "sight" — being able to see God's action in the world and to link ourselves with that creative, redemptive action, harnessing our small efforts to those of millions of others, believing that God is truly at work through us all. The more I see God's hand in it all, the more significant my little bit becomes. Besides denouncing injustice, the prophet must announce the Kingdom breaking out in our midst. Prophets are to be "energizers," persons who quicken hope because they help people see God's providential action in the world. To be such a voice and energizer, we must develop the ability to "see" God acting in our world. Contemplative silence is needed for this.[15*]

The more we see our efforts on behalf of suffering people as participating in the redemptive mission of Jesus, the more we will be willing to give ourselves generously and faithfully. We "see" the significance of what we are about. But this sight can only come when we withdraw in prayer from the fray. And so we pray as the blind man prayed, "Lord, that I may see."

It is not just our seeing that is deepened in contemplative prayer. Our hearing is also improved. The Hebrew prophets, Jesus, and Gandhi withdrew in prayer to hear more clearly what God wanted of them. No matter how busy Gandhi was, he was faithful to his hour of prayer. In 1930, when India had England on the ropes, as it were, and an aroused nation waited for directions from its spiritual as well as political leader, Gandhi withdrew in prayer. The Indian leadership had given England an ultimatum of independence by January 1, 1930, "or else." January 1 passed but Gandhi's "or else" was not revealed. Nehru and others pressed Gandhi for his plan before the Indians looked foolish, unable or unwilling to follow through on their threat. But Gandhi refused to speak. He did not have the clarity he needed. God's will was not yet clear to him.

For two months he prayed, and then the light became clear. He had heard the depth of the cry of his people as well as the voice of God. The action had to speak to the masses of the oppressed nation, an action that could harness their energy in a truly nonviolent campaign. That campaign turned out to be Gandhi's masterpiece — the salt campaign. Thousands would march to the sea, take salt illegally from the ocean, and sell it in the marketplaces, in defiance of British laws that forbade the manufacture of salt in India. Millions participated, thousands were jailed, and the campaign grew. If you saw the movie *Gandhi*, you probably remember those vivid scenes of the march, the selling of the salt, the ranks of nonviolent Indians walking into the clubs of the British soldiers guarding the Darshana Salt Works. British rule in India was finished, though it took another seventeen years before they realized it. This masterful campaign of the master of nonviolence was born of weeks of prayerful silence to hear the voice of God.[16]

We are able to discern God's will for our involvement in the world as peacemakers to the extent that we become prayerful people, silent before the Word of God in Scripture, silent before the presence of God in our heart, silent before the presence of God in others whom we read or consult in our search.

The more prayerful and centered we are, the more able we will be to perceive the portion of truth that others have, complementing our portion of truth, especially others with whom we are in conflict. The more we see that the people with whom we live, work, and struggle are God's children as much as we are, the more present we will be to them, the more able we will be to respond lovingly to them.

The more time we spend with Jesus, conversing with our friend or walking silently with him, the deeper our friendship will become. And the more convinced we will become that Jesus walks with us — across those barren deserts and raging waters into which our peacemaking can lead us. The more we are aware that Jesus has truly risen, that Jesus truly is the Lord of history, that Jesus truly walks with us, the more we will be willing to risk and perhaps even to risk it all. But that friendship with Jesus won't grow unless we take quality time apart with him.

The fruit of this contemplative venture is even richer. The result of improved hearing and sight is greater power and deeper union, not only union with Jesus, but with the whole of creation. Gandhi once defined nonviolence as "the power that manifests itself in us when we become aware of the oneness of life." The awareness that he was referring to is much more than intellectual awareness. It is closer to the biblical sense of "knowledge," which implied an intimacy associated with sexual union. When the oneness of the human family and of creation itself works itself deeply into our being, we radiate a power that is superior to all the forces of violence. There are many ways of developing this power of oneness — love force, soul force, truth force, as it has been variously called.

Fasting and other sacrificial action on behalf of others can increase our contemplative union. So will acts of service and resistance, as well as efforts to simplify our lifestyle, as we will see in later chapters. As a result of these interior efforts, Gandhi's external actions of resistance had such a loving quality about them that some of his bitterest opponents eventually were able to realize that Gandhi was not out to get them. He was truly working for their best interests as well as justice for oppressed peoples. Not that this spiritually enriched nonviolence worked immediately or worked in every case, but it worked far more than anyone thought it could. Gandhi manifested in his life and actions a profound "awareness of the oneness of life" and that was his secret. That was the source of his power. He had so given himself over to God and had become such an instrument of God's love in the world that he was "irresistible."

One of the most dramatic illustrations of this power came toward the end of Gandhi's life, his final fast unto death in the face of Hindu-Muslim violence. As Jim Douglass describes it, "Through the satyagrahi's [nonviolent lover/resister] renunciation of power along a way of radical poverty, the truth-force of the One can reassert a power which is over no one, but within all. This was the effect of Gandhi's fasting in the midst of cities being destroyed by civil and religious war, the effect of death-accepting love. Thousands of people stopped killing one another in an intensely bitter Hindu-Muslim conflict and joined in demonstrations of peace because the bonds of oneness were restored from within through the self-emptying of one who loved them all. The mystery of being's unity is a truth felt overwhelmingly through the voluntary suffering of one who loves."[17]

But we can become "irresistible" too! It starts with prayer. And there are steps we can take today.

Practical Suggestions

The first thing we can do is have a good environment for prayer. I have created a small place of beauty in our living room, a little shrine on the bottom shelf of our bookcase, where I have a crucifix, mementos from Nicaragua and elsewhere, symbols of God's creation (sand dollar, desert plaque, picture of the Pacific Ocean), a hanging plant in the corner, and a candle. I can turn my favorite chair around to face into this corner and it becomes a place of prayer for me, especially late at night, often with prayerful music in the background. We have a screened-in back porch that has a statue of Francis along with some plants, which for me is a place of prayer in warmer weather. Outside I have found special places for prayer in the St. Louis area. The Japanese Garden is my favorite, but there are places in the parks as well. Travelling offers excellent opportunities for finding God's presence in creation, especially in the mountains. There have been many such special moments for me, moments when my poetic prayerful self gets a chance to breathe deeply.

I find that writing helps my praying, whether it is writing poetry or more conversational journaling with Jesus. I used to feel compelled to write on a scheduled basis (for example, once a week for my journaling or a poem every time I went to the Japanese Garden), but now I have let go of that compulsion and write when it seems right. In any case, I have found that when I articulate in words or music the love relationship I am experiencing with Jesus, with the earth, or with people during these moments of prayerful presence, I deepen that relationship. So I encourage you to articulate in some way your experiences of contemplative union or friendship.

Finding the right times for prayer is also important. In warmer weather, sunrise is my most prayerful time, when I can sit on the back porch and rejoice in the beginning of a new day, with God's glorious sun as a sign of God's warming presence. With three teenage children rushing around at the last minute getting off to school while we try to get to the breakfast table together for at least five minutes, for me to pray in the morning means getting up well ahead of them, with some of my praying getting done as I walk the dog or do my twenty-minute morning exercise walk.

Morning prayer is important for me as an opportunity to feel "sent forth" into the day, to dedicate the whole day to God, and to ask God's help in making each moment an act of love. I pray that each encounter I have that day, whether in person, on the phone, in a letter, becomes an opportunity to love that person more fully, to be more present to that person and moment than I would normally be. In this way, I am finding that my whole day can be a prayer and St. Paul's admonition to "pray without ceasing" makes more sense. This also helps me become more mindful of each moment of the day. The famous Buddhist monk Thich Nhat Hanh says that when you wash dishes, wash dishes. Don't plan your next workshop or trip to the grocery store. Be present to the washing of the dishes. As the chief dishwasher in our family, I have taken his words to heart.

Another prayerful time for me, especially in winter, is late evening, either with the embers of the evening fire or the lighted candle in my prayer corner of the living room. What are your best times for moments of silent centering?

Sometimes books other than Scripture are helpful, though I feel the Scriptures are essential for meeting Jesus, for discovering God's will for the world.

My last suggestion is to consider a "solidarity day" each week. For me, this has generally been Friday, a day of special prayer and fasting, a day during which I spiritually "accompany" a person or group who is hurting in some way. I lift this person or group up in prayer at the beginning of the day, offer them all my struggles to let go of my appetites during the day, read about their situation, write a letter (either to them or to government officials on their behalf), or even call them to let them know how special they are to me.

Hunger pangs give me many reminders to pray during the day. I also try to do less work and focus more time and attention on the people with whom I live and work, doing little surprises for them or taking extra time to be with them. And I try to build into these days extra prayer time. I have not always been faithful to these "solidarity days," but when I have, I have been richly rewarded.

Intercessory Prayer

For Ourselves

In praying for the fulfillment of my needs, I am learning to be bolder all the time. For over eighteen years, Kathy and I have directed our Institute as a leap of faith, not one giant leap, but yearly leaps, never knowing where the necessary money and staff would come from but in the end always finding them — never more than we needed so we could have a "cushion," but never less than we needed either. I am much less hesitant about begging for help; it is often through others that God answers our prayers.

I have also learned to beg for the courage I need to go on. I have encountered some rough times over the years and have been brought to my knees. And in hindsight, I am glad for these experiences of total dependency on God's loving mercy and those people in my life who have been the instruments of this divine mercy.

For Others

Much of my prayer on my "solidarity days" is for others. The more I lift them up in prayer — those nearest me as well as those in South Africa, Central America, the Philippines, the Middle East, the Soviet Union, in nursing homes and shelters — the stronger the bonds of love grow and the more I "become aware of the oneness of life." The past few years of intense experiences in Nicaragua as well as the opportunities to be with hurting people in nursing homes, shelters, and walking the streets have helped me to become more prayerful. In the midst of these intense experiences I find myself pleading more passionately with God on behalf of the victims of violence and injustice. I can understand better now why Dorothy Day and Gandhi were such prayerful peacemakers. In the middle of it all, they "saw" more clearly, were touched more deeply, and their compassionate hearts had to cry out. That can happen to us as well. My guess is that it already has. Let's thank God for the compassion in our hearts and pray that it grows.

For Our Enemies

Intercessory prayer on behalf of our enemies seems to me to be the first step in learning how to love our enemies, which Jesus says is the test of genuine neighborly love. Dr. King's definition of *agape* is "understanding, creative, redemptive good-will for all," not just those we like. If we want to transform a hostile relationship into one more positive, if we want to put into practice Jesus' call to love our enemies, we can begin by praying for them. One friend told me of her spiritual director's advice, based on the experience of Alcoholics Anonymous, to pray daily for her enemy for two weeks and see how her attitude would be transformed. It worked.

When we pray for the well-being of someone with whom we are at odds, asking that everything we want for ourselves be given to them too, we gradually learn to appreciate their situation a little more, see a little more from their point of view, purify our own intentions, and become more willing to acknowledge our shortcomings.

Mary Evelyn Jegen, another prayerful peacemaker, has taken this insight into enemy love and applied it to the people of the Soviet Union. She writes:

> My suggestion for action to improve U.S.-Soviet relations is to find a picture of one or more persons from the Soviet Union.... I use a photograph of a five-year-old boy, Aloysha, and his three-year-old sister, Alexandra. They live in Moscow. These two children now have a place in my heart, and I pray for them in a very explicit way. They are my brother and my sister. They are God's beloved children, as I know I am. God's beloved Son was sent into our world not only for me but also for Alexandra and Aloysha. Like me they have dreams and hopes, aches and pains, loves and fears, joys and sorrows.
>
> They are our enemy. I don't let anyone tell me we have nothing against the Soviet people, but only against their government and against Communism. If we use our weapons, the government might fall, but Aloysha and Alexandra would burn and bleed and die. The truth is that if I do not resist the war-making psychology fostered by so many in our country, I am in some way implicated in the state of enmity existing between the United States and the Soviet Union.

So I must resist. But I must do more. I must stir up my faith by looking daily into the eyes of this sister and brother. I am finding that I want to know more about them and their people — their way of life, their art, their literature....

I find myself praying also for the Soviet Premier and the American President in a new way. I pray that they will take time to look deeply into each other's eyes to discover the common fear of both peoples — and to take the risk of trust. I believe this can happen because I know the perfect love of God that casts out fear. I have learned it from my little brother and sister.[18]

Mary Evelyn's insight suggests another help for our praying. She uses pictures to focus her prayer. I do too. Our family has constructed a "Shalom Box" on our dinner table. It's a shoe box on which we have taped pictures of those special persons we want to pray for — people with whom we have experienced Shalom in a special way — family members, close friends, a prisoner for whose freedom we worked for many years. These pictures have served us well as reminders for prayer each evening as we begin dinner.

Pins and chains can serve the same purpose. I know persons who have worn a bone pendant made by a former Filipino political prisoner, Santiago Alonzo. On the front of the pendant is the image of a lighted candle. On the back is the inscription — "To give light you must endure burning." Each time they put that pendant around their neck, they read the inscription and pray momentarily for Santiago and others like him and for themselves that they might be more willing to be burned a little that day in order to be God's light for the world.

Communal Prayer

Prayer Networks

A group called Evangelicals for Social Action started their prayer networks several years ago, focusing first on the need for God's reconciling love in Central America and later in South Africa. Thousands of prayerful people have committed themselves to pray daily with one another for peace and freedom in these troubled parts of our world. Knowing that my prayers are joined with others all over the world, I feel a sense of solidarity and motivation that I would not otherwise experience. The ESA has available flyers and monthly four-page updates on Central America and South Africa. The updates present the human dimensions of suffering and thus provide a concrete, personal focus for our prayer.[19]*

Prayer Support Groups

Even more helpful are the prayer support groups that provide challenge, accountability, and discernment, as well as the sense of group participation and support. When I pray intensely with a small group of like-minded disciples, we grow in insight, compassion, and courage. When we share our spiritual journeys with one another, we discover God's providential love in the lives of many and our own faith and relationship with God are thereby deepened.

The importance of community, whether it is the base communities of the Latin American church or their variations here in North America, cannot be overstated. In the words of the U.S. Roman Catholic bishops' pastoral letter on peace, "We readily recognize that we live in a world that is becoming increasingly estranged from Christian values. In order to remain a Christian, one must take a resolute stand against many commonly accepted axioms of the world.... We must develop a sense of solidarity, cemented by relationships with mature and exemplary Christians who represent Christ and his way of life" (no. 277). While they could have been more inclusive in their sense of whom we need to link with to live out our vocation as peacemakers, prophets, and disciples, they and their Methodist bishop counterparts are accurate in their estimation of what we are up against in the "powers and principalities" of this world and how we need to arm ourselves.

Prayer support groups take a variety of forms. Some have found *Sojourners* magazine an inspiring monthly resource of biblical reflection on crucial social issues and have used the magazine as the basis for their coming together in small groups. These groups not only discuss and pray over the articles in the magazine but act as a group on the issues they discuss. Many family-oriented adults have involved their whole families in family support groups, often affiliated with the Parenting for Peace and Justice Network.[20]*

Community Prayer

"Common prayer," or community prayer, is a variation of the other two forms of communal prayer. Members of religious communities in the Roman Catholic tradition gather daily for periods of group prayer, often using the Psalms, hymns, other Scripture passages, and prayers that are prayed that day all over the world. Others, not a part of these religious communities, use the same "divine office" or "breviary" or "hours" to pray in concert with others around the world. There can be a life-giving sense of solidarity in such communal experience.[21]

The ultimate form of communal prayer is liturgical worship. I explore the richness of this prayer in the next chapter.

For Reflection

Meditate on this statement from the Methodist bishops in their excellent document *In Defense of Creation:*

> Prayer is the armor of the spirit against the principalities, against the powers, against the world rulers of this present darkness (see Eph. 6:11–12). To disarm the powers, we must first disarm ourselves before God. Prayer makes us face our complicity in the world's hate and violence, our worship of false gods, our blasphemous usurpation of God's judgment. Prayer, reinforced by disciplines of fasting and penance, tempers our passions, our indulgences, and our ambitions. Prayer leads us to repentance so that we may become ministers of reconciliation. So prayer humbles. But prayer also empowers. It lifts us up to affirmation and hope, to praise and song. Prayer makes us instruments of a peace that is not ours to give. Prayer humanizes our enemies, whether Christian or non-Christian, and connects us with them in God's one world. (Pp. 84–85)

Then you might turn to a more familiar prayer, composed by one of the world's greatest contemplatives and the premier disciple of Jesus, his mother Mary. Mary's stance before God has been described in the words "Ad sum" — "here I am" — and pictured in sculpture as a woman on her knees with her hands and arms stretched out, offering herself up to God. Mary adopted that attitude in whatever she did, whether at her cousin Elizabeth's house, in flight to Egypt as a political refugee, or at the foot of

Calvary where she could only stand and offer herself and her son. For this total gift of herself to God, she has been crowned "Queen of Peace." Her hymn of praise to God is a prophetic proclamation of God's love for her, for the poor, for the whole of creation. It is prayed daily as a part of the "hour" of Vespers, and I hope it becomes a more regular part of your prayer life and mine:

> My soul magnifies the Lord and my spirit rejoices in God my Savior, because God has looked upon the lowliness of his handmaid. Yes, from this day forward all generations shall call me blessed, for the Almighty has done great things for me and holy is God's name. God's mercy reaches from age to age for those who fear God. God has shown the power of his arm and has routed the proud of heart. God has pulled down princes from their thrones and exalted the lowly. The hungry have been filled with good things and the rich sent away empty. God has come to the help of Israel his servant, mindful of his mercy — according to the promise made to Abraham and to his descendants forever. (Luke 1:46–55)

God has done wondrous things for us too. Recall those beautifully affirming lines from Psalm 139: "If I flew to the point of sunrise, or westward across the sea, your hand would still be guiding me, your right hand holding me.... It was you who created my inmost self, and put me together in my mother's womb; for all these mysteries I thank you; for the wonder of myself, for the wonder of your works." What else can we say but "thank you, God? Thank you for making your home in us and inviting us to make our home in you!"

I suggest the following as concrete next steps:

1. If you do not keep a prayer journal, consider doing so or finding another way of articulating your relationship with God, with creation, and with others. Photography adds a creative supplement to a written journal.

2. If you do not regularly pray over the Scriptures, consider doing so. If you are not sure where to start, I find chapters 5 to 7 in Matthew's Gospel and the Last Discourse of Jesus in John's Gospel (chapters 13 to 17) excellent places to pray for weeks, perhaps only a few verses at a time.

3. Read Psalm 139 in its entirety, drinking it in, savoring it, one verse at a time.

4. The writings of Henri Nouwen and Eknath Easwaren on prayer and peacemaking are excellent. If you have not read them, try one and see if either speaks to your heart as they have to so many others.[22]

5. Consider writing to Evangelicals for Social Action about their "Intercessors for Peace and Freedom" prayer networks.

6. Are you already a part of a prayer or support group? If so, are there ways you can enrich that experience? If you are not, are there possibilities through your church, or a social concerns group? Or might you ask just one other person or family about joining you for regular prayer, reflection, study, and action on issues of common concern? It only takes one other person to get started.

Chapter 5

The Lord's Supper, Our Ultimate Source of Solidarity

As THE ULTIMATE SOURCE OF ONENESS, OR SOLIDARITY, Jesus has given us his own body and blood, which we celebrate as he did, in the form of a meal. That the Supper of the Lord, or "Eucharist" ("thanksgiving"), as some Christians refer to it, is integral to peacemaking is clear from biblical sources. Jesus gave us himself as our spiritual food and drink in the context of the Jewish Passover meal. The Passover meal, described in Exodus 12:1–8, 11–14, read at the Holy Thursday liturgy, recounts God's liberation of the Jewish people from slavery and oppression. To partake of the Lord's Supper, then, is to unite in some way with God's liberating work in the world. Amos and the rest of the Hebrew prophets state clearly that ritual — worship, fasting — is meaningless unless we *live* that ritual. This means working for the liberation of the oppressed: "I reject your oblations, and refuse to look at your sacrifices of fattened cattle. Let me have no more of the din of your chanting, no more of your strumming on harps. But let justice flow like water, and integrity like an unfailing stream" (Amos 5:21–24).

In this context, it is easier to understand Paul's admonition to the people of Corinth about celebrating the Lord's Supper unworthily, that is, without "recognizing the body." "Recognizing the body" means realizing our oneness as the "body of Christ" and living out that oneness in our daily lives. As Paul writes to a divided people: "Until the Lord comes, therefore, every time you eat this bread and drink this cup, you are proclaiming his death, and so anyone who eats the bread or drinks the cup of the Lord unworthily will be behaving unworthily toward the body and blood of the Lord. Everyone is to recollect themselves before eating this bread and drinking this cup; because a person

45

who eats and drinks without recognizing the body is eating and drinking their own condemnation" (2 Cor. 11:26–30).

Not only does the Lord's Supper symbolize our oneness as the body of Christ and send us forth to realize this oneness more fully through our action, but it also is the source of that oneness and the grace we need to live it out. No wonder peacemakers like Dorothy Day celebrated the Lord's Supper daily. Others do it weekly; still others less frequently. Many women, especially Roman Catholics, experience deep pain in official celebrations of the Lord's Supper, because of male dominance in the leadership and language of the worship. Our commitment, in my opinion, should include working to make the Lord's Supper a more consistent symbol of the unity and equality of women and men in our churches.

Here I share my experience as a Roman Catholic who has celebrated the Eucharist daily during different periods of my life. I have also worshipped and preached in Protestant churches over the years. And while I feel comfortable and enriched worshipping in many different faith traditions, I am most at home "at Mass." My reflections on the moments of the Lord's Supper parallel the "order of worship" of the Mass. But because these moments are part of the liturgical experience of most Christians who celebrate the Lord's Supper, I hope to speak to all who share in that Supper.

The Lord's Supper

The Penitential Rite

Most celebrations of the Lord's Supper begin with a penitential rite in which we confess our sinfulness. Generally we think of our own personal sinfulness, but we need to think of our sinfulness as a people as well. We need to confess our participation in the sinfulness of our community, nation, and species and beg God's forgiveness and mercy on us all. "Social sin" needs to be confessed — the sin embedded in institutions and societal attitudes and practices. "Lord, have mercy on us" for our corporate greed and national wastefulness as well as for our personal desire for comfort and convenience. "Lamb of God, you take away the sin of the world" — our closing hospitals and schools in poor areas, building ever more destructive weapons while hunger increases, condoning the death of the unborn or the execution of prisoners, imprisoning and torturing people for their political or religious convictions, enticing the poor to buy luxuries for the sake of profit — "have mercy on us." Yes, Lord, on us, all of us, for we are one family, one body. This is our first opportunity in worship to bring to mind the suffering of our brothers and sisters, to unite with them in their suffering, to realize our complicity in that suffering, and to beg forgiveness.

Glory and Praise

Most Sunday liturgies include what Catholics call the "Gloria," a hymn that begins with the angels' proclamation of praise and joy at the birth of Jesus: "Glory to God in the highest and peace to God's people on earth." Our God is the Creator of the universe, the infinite, the transcendent, the totally "Other," and so we acknowledge that mystery, that awesome reality, by addressing God as "Lord God, heavenly King, almighty God and Father [Mother, Creator God]. We worship you, we give you thanks, we praise you for your glory!" The whole universe is a hymn of glory to God's creative, infinite love and beauty. We lift up this creation as well as our voices in singing God's praise.

Then we turn to Jesus, "the only son of God," and acknowledge him both as Lord and lamb — "Lord, God, lamb of God, you take away the sin of the world, have mercy on us." Another chance to beg for healing for our world and for ourselves and to realize that Jesus is Lord precisely because he submitted himself completely to God's will and give himself up for us as a "lamb led to the slaughter."

And because "he emptied himself... even to accepting death, death on a cross, God raised him high and gave him the name that is above all other names, so that all beings... should bend the knee at the name of Jesus and every tongue should acclaim Jesus Christ as Lord..." (Phil. 2:6–11). And now that Jesus sits at the right hand of God, we can confidently ask him to receive our prayers, for he alone is the "holy one," he alone is "Lord." He is to be our Lord, our only Lord. We cannot serve two masters. We must not worship other gods — a standard of living, a nation state, an ideology like capitalism or communism. Jesus is to be our Lord, him alone are we to serve, with our total selves.

Liturgy of the Word

The Scriptures are essential for the insight and inspiration needed in our lives as prophets, peacemakers, and disciples. Responding to those readings selected by the church each week puts us in touch with the whole body of Christ as well as with sources from our Jewish heritage. Particularly if these readings relate to peacemaking and discipleship, we can use them as the basis of our reflection and prayer for the whole week.[23]*

Our Gifts — "the Offertory"

While our monetary gifts are important, our lives are much more important gifts to bring to the altar. Here we get another chance to "recognize the body" by placing on the paten or plate, along with the bread that is to become the Body of Christ, all the other members of that body. We can unite with the bread all who are symbolized in that bread, in all their constructive efforts that day or week, all our efforts to build up the body of Christ around the world. We can unite with Jesus' efforts all that our sisters and brothers around the world are doing to rebuild cities, rebuild lives, striving to make relationships work and make institutions work for people; members of our one body struggling to overcome hunger and feed their families; brothers and sisters learning, sharing, caring for one another and for the earth. We can unite all these efforts — particularly ones we can concretely visualize or are personally involved in — to Jesus' efforts, asking him to transform them, as we lift them up to God as our act of unity, praise, thanksgiving, and commitment. For we place ourselves on that paten as well — all our talents, our activities, our loves, our whole self — and ask to be transformed into ever more loving instruments of God's loving action in the world, to truly become God's "melody."

And into the cup, along with the wine and water, we can pour our own blood and that of other members of the body of Christ — the blood that will be spilled this day or week around the world — in prisons, in broken homes and lives, in poverty and oppression, on battlefields, wherever racism and sexism and repression stunt peoples' lives. United to the wine that will become the blood of Jesus, our suffering can be redemptive and not spilled in vain. This, too, we unite to Jesus' total gift of himself to God on our behalf.

Consecration

After joining the angels in their acclamation of God's utter holiness (see Isa. 6:1–3) and the Hebrew children in their "hosannas" to Jesus who comes in the name of the Lord, we focus on our gifts and implore God to "let your Spirit come upon these gifts to make them holy, so that they may become for us the Body of Christ." The bread is broken, as Jesus' body was broken, so that we will be made whole again. The wine is Jesus' blood spilled for all, so that sins might be forgiven. Jesus' death is the sign of God's "new covenant" of Shalom with us. What more could God give us to show us how much we are loved! And then the worshipping community through its worship leaders lifts up these gifts to God, as Jesus did at his last supper. As Jesus instructed us, we do the same in memory of him and his total giving of himself.

Then we pray "that from East to West a perfect offering may be made to Your name, O Lord." My trip to the Soviet Union in the summer of 1988 brought this prayer to life for me in a new way. I helped to celebrate a thousand years of Christianity in what is now the Soviet Union, a celebration marking the baptism of Prince (and also Saint) Vladimir and his people in the Kievan Rus (the area around the city of Kiev in the Ukraine, which is today one of the fifteen republics in the U.S.S.R.). I encountered thousands of deeply faithful, worshipping Christians of all ages and sensed a resurgence of religious fervor in the Soviet Union that many other visitors have similarly experienced. "From East to West" we are one family, one body of Christ. And we can lift up our Eastern brothers and sisters in a special way at this moment in our worship.

The Lord's Prayer

We hold up our gifts and pray that "through him [Jesus], with him, and in him, in the unity of the Holy Spirit, all glory and honor is yours, almighty Father [Mother, Creator God], now and forever. Amen!" Thus we prepare for receiving Jesus in Communion by reciting the prayer that Jesus himself taught us, a prayer rich for peacemakers.

"Our Father [Mother, Creator God]...." "Our": the whole human species, in fact the whole of creation, is encompassed in this tiny word. I close my eyes and experience a momentary flash of oneness that I pray permeates my spirit. "Father [Mother, Creator God]" — "Abba" is the Hebrew word, closer to "Daddy" than "Father." How intimately God relates to us! Recall the tender language of Psalm 139, or the words of Isaiah 49:15, where God says that even if a mother could forget her child, there is no way God could forget us. God's love for us is more tender than that of a mother for her baby at her breast.

"Thy Kingdom come": how pleadingly we can say those words. "Please, God, may Your Kingdom come! Come! and may we be your willing instruments in that coming."

"Thy will be done on earth as it is in heaven": another chance to plead. "Please, may your will be done, your will for Shalom, here on earth as fully as it is being realized in heaven. And, again, may we be more willing instruments of your will."

"Give us this day our daily bread": a chance to plead for our own needs, but especially for the hungry and homeless of our world. I try to visualize the people I have met in the shelters I visit, as well as images of hungry people in refugee camps in Central America, the Middle East, Africa, and Southeast Asia. I beg for them in terms as specific as possible.

"And forgive us our trespasses [sins, debts] as we forgive those who trespass against us": a dangerous prayer, for it asks God to treat us the same as we treat those who have offended us. I recall people with whom I have been in conflict and remind myself of my need to be forgiving, to love unconditionally, because that is how God loves me.

"And lead us not into temptation, but deliver us from evil": we can pray that we do not give in to our fears, selfishness, and attachments; that we do not compromise with evil, with the powers and principalities of this world; and that religious and political leaders as well as the rest of us resist these evils, these dragons of our time. I think momentarily of the woman in the Book of Revelation and her incredible courage and hope in the face of the dragon and ask for similar courage and hope.

"For Thine is the Kingdom, the power, and the glory, forever and ever": here is our opportunity to reassert that these all belong to God, not us. God's Kingdom of Shalom is not a kingdom "of this world," as Jesus asserted before Pilate (John 18:36). It is a Kingdom God very much intends to realize, but through each of us as the agents of that Kingdom. And the power? It's not from us but from God, the power of God's Spirit alive and active in our hearts and our world. The "glory"? It does not belong to us, but to God. "Let your light shine before all, so that they may see the good that you do and give glory to God" (Matt. 5:14–16). When we preach, formally as part of worship or informally as part of sharing our faith with others, we are to preach Christ Jesus, not ourselves (2 Cor. 4:5).

Praying for Peace

Once again we address Jesus as the "lamb of God who takes away the sins of the world." We ask for mercy for ourselves as sinners and for the "social sins" of our world. In the spirit of the Hebrew prophets, we can beg that our sinful world be spared God's wrath, that we be spared what we deserve, that somehow the consequences of our disregard for the earth and of our resort to violence to solve personal, community, and international problems will not be as disastrous as they should be. And we beg for peace: "grant us peace."

We pray for "peace and unity" for our church; so much reconciliation needs to take place within our church, our local congregations as well as nationally and internationally. Then we ourselves are offered "peace": "May the peace of Christ be with you." After returning that salutation to the worship leader, we share peace with those around us. "Passing the peace," or "the kiss of peace," as it is variously called, is a wonderful opportunity to experience our oneness, solidarity, Shalom right up close, with those physically around us. If there are members of our family or our congregation with whom we need to be reconciled, here is an opportunity for a little of that to happen. Before we receive Jesus in Communion as a sign of our unity, we take a step toward reconciling ourselves with those sisters and brothers with whom are at odds. Jesus made it clear that we should leave our gifts at the altar and go to those with whom we need to be reconciled and only then return to the altar to offer sacrifice. Recall, too, Paul's warning about receiving Communion without "recognizing the body."

Communion

What a sacred opportunity this should be for us: the chance to receive Jesus, to take him into our person, to become more like him, to be better able to say that "it is now no longer I who live but Christ who lives in me." But it is even more than an experience of intense union with the person Jesus. It is the ultimate moment of unifying ourselves (or better, being unified) with the whole human family, with the whole of creation. In receiving Jesus in Communion, we taken into ourselves Jesus as he now is — *the whole body of Christ.* When we say yes to Jesus in Communion, we are saying yes to the whole human family united in Jesus. We can commit ourselves to deepening this realization of the oneness of the human family in our hearts and to working for a fuller realization of this oneness in the world.

And the grace to make and carry out this commitment comes from Communion as well. The Eucharist is not just the symbol of our unity, but the source of that unity. As I learned as a child, because it is a "sacrament," the Eucharist "effects what it signifies." As Paul tells us, "the fact that there is only one loaf means that, though there are many of us, we form a single body because we all have a share in this one loaf" (1 Cor. 10:17). Singing during Communion enriches the communitarian dimension of the Eucharist. If there are also moments of silence after Communion, there can be an opportunity to recommit ourselves to the building up of the body of Christ in concrete ways.

Commissioning and Dismissal

Catholic liturgies conclude with the words, "The Mass has ended; go in peace, to love and serve the Lord." Whatever the words of the dismissal, we are invited to go forth and take the Shalom we received in the liturgy and share it with others. Each of us is called to serve the Lord. We have different people to go to, different things to say, but we are all clearly sent forth to live our Communion, to embody our worship, to turn our ritual into practice, as the Hebrew prophets, Jesus, Paul, and other prophets have emphatically directed us.

I have been part of the commissioning of ministers to go forth on behalf of the entire community to those in need. In some cases, this was a commissioning of the "Eucharistic ministers," those who were to bring Communion to the shut-ins of the congregation. In other cases, it was the commissioning of the "care givers," those who ministered more broadly to the needy of the community. The point is the same. Our worship is not complete until we go forth and share what we have received, become God's melodies of peace for our world. Recall Francis's Peace Prayer, "Lord, make me an instrument of your peace."

The Liturgical Year

My conviction has grown over the years that the more we integrate our peacemaking or social action efforts with the seasons and feasts of the liturgical year, the more meaning they have, the deeper our commitment grows, the more integrated our lives become.

Advent and Christmas

The Christmas season is an ideal time to focus on simplicity and service. The symbol of the manger is clear and very much a part of the life of most Christian families. Not as a king robed in splendor did Jesus come. No, he came poor and homeless. Jesus came to serve and not to be served. Our own family Advent tradition revolves around this symbol of simplicity and service. Several evenings each week we gather at our homemade manger. The children still take turns lighting the candles, one for each week of Advent. We reflect on the day that has passed and on some way each of us was able to be of service to someone else. As each of us shares this service experience, we place a piece of straw in our crib to make a softer place for Jesus to lie. Because of the Holy Family's experience of homelessness ("no room in the inn") and exile as refugees (fleeing to Egypt to escape the reach of Herod, who wanted to kill his potential kingly rival), we might seek out ways we can provide hospitality during this season or help refugee families in our community. Finally, Jesus' coming as "the prince of peace," with January 1st as a day of prayer for world peace, can give our peacemaking actions additional meaning at this time of year.[24*]

Lent

In Lent the focus is Jesus' passion, relived in the world today. Members of the body of Christ suffer from neglect, greed, and oppression. Lent is an especially appropriate time for responding to their needs. Lent is a time of repentance; hunger, racism, and other forms of injustice are blatant expressions of human sinfulness. Holy Week is when Jesus gave us the Lord's Supper;

neglect and oppression are a denial of the oneness that this Supper proclaims. Lent is the time for uniting with the passion of Jesus, as it is being relived in our time.

In calling us to repentance, Lent provides an ideal opportunity to respond to the passion of Jesus relived in the suffering members of the body of Christ. As Veronica wiped the face of Jesus and Simon helped him carry his cross (actions remembered in the traditional "Stations of the Cross"), we can similarly respond to hurting people. For years, our family has done our "stations in the city," places in our community where the passion of Christ is being relived in the suffering of others.

One Good Friday in particular was a special experience for our family and our understanding of Lent. At breakfast, we explained to the children why we had decided to withhold a symbolic $12 from our federal tax payment — as a protest against increases in military spending and decreases in spending for human needs. The human-need examples we used were simple ones that the children (then four, six, and eight) were already familiar with and ones we planned to see later in the day (since then, the children have helped us identify what places we should visit and needs we should respond to).

That afternoon we left work early to spend an hour with the children following the path of Jesus' passion through St. Louis. First, we went to rubble piles next to our office that weeks before had been homes. Then we stopped at the nearby parish school about to close. The children noticed the colorful Easter pictures in the windows and commented on how much the students probably liked their school. What a shame, we replied, that homes are destroyed and schools are closed because tax dollars are going for Trident submarines rather than neighborhood rehabilitation and education.

The next stop was the children's hospital where David had recently undergone surgery. Each child had decided to bring a book to leave in the playroom. They had talked about how children awaiting surgery often feel afraid and lonely. So their books were a response to Christ's suffering in other children. Then, suckers in hand (from David's nurse), we headed off to the post office, where we all signed our tax protest letters and mailed them to the President, the IRS, and our congressional representatives. There we talked about how important it is to try to change the situations that contribute to poverty, as well as to respond to people's immediate needs (though at four years of age, Theresa was more concerned about how to spell her name).

The last stop on our short journey was the county jail, where a young man we had gotten to know had been waiting trial for two years. Since the children were tired, we switched plans from writing individual letters to writing a group letter to Gerald, which we all signed and delivered to a jail guard. We ended the hour with a prayer for Gerald and his mother — two people experiencing Christ's passion in their lives.[25]

For the past eight years we have been making our "stations in the city" with other families. Some families do them as part of a group from their congregation; others do them with community peace and justice groups.

Fasting and prayer are especially appropriate as Lenten practices. In fasting, we can voluntarily take on, in a tiny act of solidarity, the suffering of those who hunger involuntarily. Family efforts to simplify meals and skip snacks and "happy hours" can free up money for both restocking a local food pantry or supporting hunger groups — like Bread for the World or Oxfam-America — that are working for social change.

In prayer, symbol and ritual are important. A bowl of earth with a candle placed on the dinner table is a sign of repentance. On Ash Wednesday we receive a cross of dust or ashes on our foreheads as a sign that we are from the earth and will return to the earth (Joel 2:12–19). The earth is also a sign of the ground into which the seed must fall if it is to bear fruit (John 12:24–25). And the earth is a sign of food and the fruitfulness of God's creation, for the earth is the source of food. Our prayer might be to be more willing to sacrifice ourselves and become a source of food for others. As we light the candle, we can remind ourselves of Jesus' presence as the "Light of the world" from whose light we become lights for the world too. Recall the inscription on the back of Santiago Alonzo's bone pendant: "to give light, you must endure burning."

Easter

Our hope is rooted in the Resurrection of Jesus. Jesus truly lives. Sin has been overcome. We are a saved people. We have already begun to live God's Kingdom of Shalom. Yet we know that the Kingdom is not yet fully realized. Hunger, racism, militarism, and all the other dragons are very real and present. It is the Resurrection of Jesus that guarantees the ultimate fruitfulness of our efforts to confront these dragons. If the seed falls into the ground and dies, it will bear fruit.

During this season, it is appropriate to focus on social action that has a strong "Easter flavor." This means hope, and the action that inspires the most hope in me is creating new ways of living and alternative institutions. Such efforts require deep hope, and are themselves a sign of hope for others. They say that things can be different, that we can create a different life for ourselves. This year at Easter our family will celebrate in a special way the reality of Easter hope witnessed by the faith of our prisoner friend, Gerald, and his mother. After twelve years, he was finally granted a retrial and found not guilty. Today he is back with his family, employed, and witnessing to his Muslim faith that carried him through the ordeal.

As a symbol of Easter hope and call to prayerful reflection in this season, we can use that Lenten bowl of earth. During Lent, seeds can be planted in that earth, so that they blossom during Easter time. But any Easter flowers can stimulate our hope and prayer.

Pentecost

Jesus sent his Spirit to transform his disciples and ultimately the world. Though few in number, the disciples touched many and the Gospel spread. That same Spirit works in us today. As the 1971 Synod of Roman Catholic bishops put it: "The power of the Spirit, who raised Christ from the dead, is continuously at work in the world. Through the generous sons and daughters of the church likewise, the People of God is present in the midst of the poor and of those who suffer oppression and persecution; it lives in its own flesh and its own heart the Passion of Christ and bears witness to His Resurrection" (*Justice in the World*, Part IV). To celebrate Pentecost, then, is to allow the Spirit to work through us, through our efforts to help transform the world: "Come, Holy Spirit, fill the hearts of your faithful and enkindle in us the fire of your love. Send forth your Spirit, Lord, and we will be recreated and you will renew (through us) the face of the earth."

Special Feasts

During the course of the liturgical year, there are feasts and other days of commemoration that can provide spiritual support for our peacemaking efforts and serve as days of special prayer, recommitment, and action. These include:

- January 1 is a day of prayer for world peace.

- January 15 is the birthday of Martin Luther King (and a U.S. national holiday).

- February 14 is the feast of St. Valentine, a special day to remember people in prison, as Valentine was when he was befriended by the daughter of his jailor. His thank-you note to her was signed, "Your Valentine."

- March 24 is the anniversary of the 1980 assassination of Archbishop Oscar Romero of El Salvador.

- May 1 is the feast of St. Joseph the Worker, father of Jesus, and patron of workers.

- Yom HaShoah, Holocaust Memorial Day, is observed in the week after Passover.

- Memorial Day, the last Monday in May, is a day for people of faith to recommit themselves to working for alternatives to war, and to remember the victims of mass human violence around the world.

- "Corpus Christi," a special Sunday shortly after Pentecost to celebrate the "Body of Christ," is another opportunity to integrate this theme into our work for Shalom.

- June 5 is World Environment Day.

- July 28 is the feast of St. Vladimir in the Soviet Union. While it is generally not celebrated in North America, it could be a day of special efforts toward building bridges with the people of the Soviet Union.

- August 6 is the anniversary of the bombing of Hiroshima.

- August 9 is the anniversary of the bombing of Nagasaki, and is also the anniversary of the death of Franz Jaegerstatter, the Austrian conscientious objector whom Hitler had executed in 1943.

- September 8 is the feast of the birth of Mary, the Mother of Jesus.

- September 12 is the anniversary of the death of Steve Biko, young Black consciousness leader in South Africa, killed by the apartheid government.

- October 2 is the anniversary of Gandhi's birth in 1862.

- October 4 is the anniversary of Francis's death in 1226.

- October 24 is a day of celebration of the United Nations.

- *Sukkoth* is a seven-day Jewish holiday celebrated right after Yom Kippur in October or November. As a celebration of our connectedness with the earth and our brief sojourn on earth, as a thanksgiving for the harvest and a pledge to share its fruits with others, and as a commemoration of the Jewish wilderness experience, Jewish families build a hut, for a hut served their people as a temporary dwelling in the fields while gathering the harvest for winter. Today it's called *sukkah shalom*, a *sukkah* of peace, a hut made of new cuttings to remind us of our temporary connectedness with the earth.

- November 8 and 29 are the anniversaries of the birth (1900) and death (1980) of Dorothy Day.

- December 2 is the anniversary of the assassinations of four U.S. religious women missionaries in El Salvador (Ita Ford, Maura Clark, Jean Donovan, Dorothy Kazel).

- December 12 is the feast of Our Lady of Guadalupe, patron of the poor of Mexico and all the Americas.

- December 28 is the feast of the "Holy Innocents," babies killed by Herod in his effort to kill the baby Jesus; it is a day to remember the "holy innocents" of every era, the children who are the first victims of war and poverty.

The importance of celebrating such days has been made clear to me over the years as I ask people to trace their personal faith journeys and identify those pivotal experiences that have brought them to where they are today. Invariably every person names other people who have inspired them by their willingness to risk for the Gospel. Placing ourselves in relationship to such people can inspire us to further risk-taking. I have tried to read at least one biography of such a person each year, often during Lent, and I look for videos throughout the year. If you have not read such a book recently, consider picking one and set aside a time when you will be able to be present to its challenge.[26*]

For Reflection

1. In the reflections on the Lord's Supper what touched you most? Can you incorporate it into your worship experiences, even share it with others?

2. On those days we are not able to worship communally, we can still lift up the world and the whole body of Christ, as French theologian and paleontologist Pierre Teilhard de Chardin did. He writes:

Once again, Lord, I have no bread, no wine, no altar; therefore, I, your priest, will make the whole earth my altar and on it will offer you all the labors and sufferings of the world. . . . What are this paten and this chalice of mine? They are the depths of a soul laid utterly open to all the energies which in a moment will rise up from the earth's corners and meet together and together mount towards the Spirit. Give me then, Lord, to call to mind, and to hold mystically present before my eyes, all those whom the light is now awakening to a new day. . . . I beg you, Lord, accept this all-embracing Host which your whole creation, moved by your magnetism, now offers you at this dawn of a new day.[27]

3. Think over your recent worship experiences. What has given you a greater sense of solidarity with the body of Christ? What aspects of your worship experiences would you like to see changed? Can you do anything about these changes?

4. If your current worship experiences are not leading you to a greater sense of solidarity with Jesus and his whole Body, can you provide such experiences in your home or place of work or with people with whom you are socially or politically involved? Would a "retreat" experience be good for you in the near future? I have found a yearly retreat more and more essential. Also helpful to me has been a spiritual director and a "soul brother," someone who can help guide me in my faith journey.

5. What is the next season of the liturgical year? Are there ways you can integrate your service or social action activities more fully with the traditions of this season? If you live with others, are there ways you can involve them?

Chapter 6

Living on Gospel Terms: A Lifestyle of Solidarity

Solidarity with god, with the human family, and with the whole of creation, is very difficult if not impossible, if we live immersed in material comforts. Reducing the amount of material goods we depend on, as well as our attachment to them, can help us become more single-minded in living our faith and responding to the call of discipleship. We need to root out the obstacles in our lives that keep us from risking and from loving more deeply. Being too comfortable can also dull our sense of urgency and passion for justice. We are called to "hunger and thirst for justice," not just dabble at it in our spare time. Further, learning to live on less can help us identify more fully with the majority of the human family who have little in the way of material goods. Finally, the self-discipline involved in simplifying our lives can help us become more fit instruments of solidarity. Committing ourselves to discipleship demands a willingness to take risks and to persevere for a lifetime. Spiritual, mental, and physical stamina are essential.

The Gospels are emphatic:

- "Do not store up treasures for yourselves on earth, where moths and woodworms destroy them and thieves can break in and steal. But store up treasures for yourselves in heaven, where neither moth nor woodworms destroy them and thieves cannot break in and steal. For where your treasure is, there will your heart be also" (Matt. 6:19–21).

- "No one can be the slave of two masters; they will either hate the first and love the second, or treat the first with respect and the second with scorn. You cannot be the slave of both God and money" (Matt. 6:24).

- "Look at the birds in the sky. They do not sow or reap or gather into barns; yet your heavenly Parent feeds them. Are you not worth much more than they are?... Think of the lilies of the field.... So do not worry; do not say, 'what are we to eat? what are we to drink? how are we to be clothed?' It is pagans who set their hearts on all these things. Your heavenly Parent

60

> knows you need them all. Set your hearts on God's Kingdom first, and on
> God's righteousness, and all these other things will be given you as well"
> (Matt. 6:25–33).

How often have we heard these words! How often have we
dismissed them as unrealistic. "Lilies of the field" — is Jesus
serious? "Birds in the sky" — isn't that a little irresponsible?
Maybe birds can fly around and pick up the food they need, but
that is no model for responsible parenthood, for fidelity on the
job, for developing our talents.

Do you find yourself raising objections: "We have to be more
practical and plan for the future. How will my children get the
education they deserve? Who will provide for our retirement?"
What does Jesus want of us? We live in a society that does not
provide quality health care and education unless you can pay for
it. There is no guarantee of a job in the U.S. People have to
make it on their own. Adequate housing is not regarded as a
right. Neither is an adequate diet, despite food stamp programs.
The U.S. may have "social security," but there is no real social
and economic security for the poor, the elderly, for anyone who
is not wealthy. The "safety net" is anything but safe. We have
many reasons for worrying about the future.

I can easily apply these scriptural passages to people whose
major concern in life is to "get ahead," perhaps at any cost; to
people for whom consumption is their god. They often burn
themselves out at work, pay little attention to their families, buy
an endless string of unnecessary things. But that's not most of us.
And yet we *are* tempted to get ahead, to buy nice things, to live
in nice neighborhoods, with nice houses and nice furnishings.
We like comfort when we can get it. And some of us get it often.
When I take time to think about Jesus' words, I am often troubled,
and my guess is that you are too.

Is this what Jesus wants of us — "to sell all we have and give
it to the poor and come follow him"? Maybe we could sell a
few things, but is Jesus serious about selling everything? What
does he want of us? To do whatever it takes to follow him all the
way? To set our hearts first on God's Kingdom of Shalom? To
lay down our lives for our friends? What does it mean to follow
Jesus, to give the Kingdom of God our whole heart, to lay down
our lives for our friends, to "sell all" that would compromise such

a commitment? And how do we do this in a society that does not provide security for its lilies or birds or people?

You are probably like me, unwilling to take drastic measures like Francis of Assisi. You probably do not anticipate being knocked to the ground as Paul was. You are probably comfortable moving one step at a time. Here we'll look at ways to take a few steps in the direction of living more on Gospel terms than on society's or the bank's. I have discovered these through a combination of three "P"s — prayer, principles, and practice. I start with prayer, understood as listening to God with silent and open hearts, letting the Word of God penetrate our hearts. But I see it including joining with others in struggling with Jesus' challenging call. In prayer we learn more about God's Kingdom of Shalom and find the courage to embrace God's will and follow Jesus more fully. Our prayer will be enlightened as we take practical steps to get rid of the baggage that keeps us from following Jesus. In prayer, both private and communal, we discover the principles that guide our practical steps. Here we'll look at four: a preferential option for the poor; connecting with the earth; simplifying our lives; and finding support.

"Preferential Option for the Poor"

Listen to our contemporary prophets:

- "In the face of each poor person, I see the face of Jesus" (Mother Teresa).

- "Several times I have decided to leave El Salvador. I almost could except for the children, the poor, bruised victims of this insanity. Who would care for them? Whose heart could be so staunch as to favor the reasonable thing in a sea of their tears and loneliness? Not mine, dear friend, not mine" (Jean Donovan, quoted in *Salvador Witness*, p. 212).

- "God's love encompasses all people; but God has demonstrated a special concern for poor people, the needy, the helpless, and the oppressed and acted on their behalf to bring justice. God calls the church to commit itself to be an advocate with and on behalf of the poor, the powerless, the victims of injustice" (the 196th General Assembly of the Presbyterian Church USA, *Christian Faith and Economic Justice*, 1984, no. 29.324).

- "The example of Jesus poses a number of challenges to the contemporary church. It imposes a prophetic mandate to speak for those who have no one to speak for them, to be a defender of the defenseless, who in biblical terms are the poor. It also demands a compassionate vision that enables the church to see things from the side of the poor and powerless, and to assess lifestyle, policies and social institutions in terms of their impact on the poor.... Finally, and most radically, it calls for an emptying of self, both individually and corporately, that allows the church to experience the power of God in the midst of poverty and powerlessness" (U.S. Catholic Bishops in their 1986 pastoral letter, *Economic Justice for All*, no. 52).

Both these church reflections provide contemporary comment on what the Hebrew prophets proclaimed in unambiguous terms. To cite but one passage from Jeremiah, where he compares the current king of Israel with the king's father: "Your father ate and drank, like you, but he practiced honesty and integrity, so all went well for him. He used to examine the cases of the poor and needy, then all went well. Is not that what it means to know me? — it is Adonai who speaks" (Jer. 22:15–16). Taking up the cause of the poor is what it means to *know* God. *God cannot be known apart from active solidarity with the poor.*

On what terms are we to make decisions about economic matters? We are to do so "in terms of their impact on the poor." Mother Teresa and Jean Donovan have both given their lives for their friends, God's special ("preferential option") friends, the poor. So must we, somehow. Compassionate service is the first way — devoting some part of our heart and treasure to one-to-one time with the poor. This can be done in a nursing home, a shelter for the homeless, a food pantry. Hospitality — opening our hearts and home to others — can involve our whole family, especially if our home is involved. Hospitality is a whole orientation of our person — being available to others. Making space in our heart and home for a troubled teen, an overnight visitor, a lonely neighbor, a refugee, or one of our children's friends is an appropriate and important response to Jesus' call to the spiritual as well as the corporal works of mercy (see Matt. 25:31–46).

But we can connect with the poor in other ways and live and work sacrificially in a way that alleviates their poverty. Lifestyle connections are as unlimited as our imaginations:

• *A "world bank"* on our dinner table can remind us to eat sacrificially and to share the savings with those who are hungry.[28] The "Operation Rice Bowl" box (from Catholic Relief Services) and similar campaigns from Church World Service and other Protestant outreach programs provide similar reminders, especially appropriate during Lent.

• *Public transportation* in some areas provides an experience of solidarity with the poor, for that is generally their only form of transportation. It can be an experience of inconvenience that the poor live with daily and that most of us convenience-oriented persons do anything to avoid. Public transportation is the North American urban counterpart of Gandhi's spinning wheel. Gandhi spent an hour a day at his spinning wheel so that his body as well as his mind and heart would experience the life of the economically poor. He also wanted to show them how they could provide for their own clothing needs, rather than rely on the British. Gandhi felt it essential to take on the life of the poor if he were going to be "one" with them. "Urban plunges," living on a welfare budget for a month, spending a weekend in a shelter for the homeless provide important momentary experiences that can touch our hearts and minds.

But perhaps there needs to be something more regular in our lives that connects us with the poor in ways that nurture our sense of solidarity. Besides public transportation, what are some other possibilities? Clinics rather than private doctors? Public rather than private education? Public vs. private recreational activities and facilities? Are there others that make more sense for your circumstances? One friend of mine related how she felt the need for what she called a "zone of discomfort" as a way of identifying with the poor. She and her daughters chose to replace the portable air conditioner in their trailer home with a fan. Later they decided to share the dollar savings with the poor.

• By *eating "connectedly"* we can make explicit our food connections with the poor and turn these external links into bonds of internal solidarity. The decision to boycott grapes, for example, can be an opportunity for solidarity with U.S. farm workers and their families suffering from poisonous pesticides. A picture of a farm worker on the dinner table, perhaps as part of a "Shalom Box" (see above, p. 40), can remind our household of our connection with these providers of our food. Buying directly from local farmers at a farmers' market, rather than always from giant supermarkets, provides another opportunity for solidarity.

If your economic situation is like mine — middle-class — or if you are better off financially, you will probably find the following reflection on voluntary poverty quite challenging. I do, every time I go back to it. It is from Gustavo Gutiérrez, a deeply prayerful Peruvian theologian most famous for his book, *A Theology of Liberation*, in which he writes about the redemptive character of voluntary poverty, the ways poverty helps create a oneness with the human family, especially with those members who are suffering. It is not that Gutiérrez sees poverty as ideal, or even as good. On the contrary, he is reminding us to work *against poverty.* Nor is he suggesting that those of us who are not poor "play at" being poor. Rather, he challenges us to let go of the privileges we have *at the expense of the poor.* Poverty, he says,

> has a redemptive value. If the ultimate cause of human exploitation and alienation is selfishness, the deepest reason for voluntary poverty is love of neighbor.... It is not a question of idealizing poverty, but rather of taking it on as it is — an evil — to protest against it and to struggle to abolish it. As Ricoeur says, you cannot really be with the poor unless you are struggling against poverty. Because of this solidarity — which must manifest itself in action, a style of life, a break with one's social class — one can also help the poor and exploited to become aware of their exploitation and seek liberation from it. Christian poverty, an expression of love, is solidarity with the poor and is a protest against poverty.... It is a poverty which means taking on the sinful condition of people to liberate them from sin and all its consequences.[29]

When we find the courage to relinquish some of our privileges and to join with the poor in concrete action to challenge economic, political, and church institutions to change unjust practices and policies, we experience a special solidarity. We are taking another step in embracing Jesus' special love for the poor (see Luke 4:16–18) and that radical "emptying of self" that the Catholic bishops identified as essential.

Gandhi was clear in the explanation of his half-nakedness while in jail: "If I want to be one with the people of India, I must live like them." How can we apply this to our lives? I think immediately of my clothes closet and how many of the items I really need or have even worn in the last year. Such questioning always leads me to pull a few more items to share with those who have so much less. I recall vividly the statement of St. Ambrose that "you are not making a gift of your possessions to the poor. You are handing over to them what is theirs. For what has been given in common for the use of all, you have arrogated to yourself. The world is given to all, and not only to the rich."[30] Even more graphic are similar statements attributed to St. Basil, another early Father of the Church: "The bread which you do not use is the bread of the hungry. The garment hanging in your wardrobe is the garment of the one who is naked. The shoes you do not wear are the shoes of the one who is barefoot."

Friends of ours have an "exchange system" for their purchases. Whenever possible, they circulate out of their house to someone in need an item comparable to each new item they bring into their house. This works especially well with clothing, with reading material, with toys, sometimes with appliances and other larger household items. It doesn't reduce our standard of living, but it keeps something of a lid on it.

Relinquishing privileges, especially those we have at the expense of the poor, means downward mobility, something quite counter to the prevailing culture and thus difficult for many of us caught in that culture. The "good life" does look and taste good. It is hard to let go of it. Other "experiments with truth," to put it in Gandhian terms, are to let go of luxury foods and drink, buy more second-hand clothing, get used furniture, learn to repair more things, participate in exchanges in our neighborhood or church. Can we occasionally use our own labor, as in baking bread or washing dishes by hand, rather than always choosing labor-saving and time-saving appliances and foods?

Henri Nouwen, Richard Rohr, and Jim Douglass suggest that relinquishing privileges and downward mobility can move us to deeper levels inside ourselves.[31*] Besides letting go of things, are we willing to let go of the need to be productive (or "relevant"), the need to be recognized and acclaimed (or "spectacular"), and the need to be in control (or "powerful")? Nouwen sees these as the three temptations of Jesus confronting us in twentieth-century affluent North America. Are we willing to identify with the humble Jesus of Philippians 2:6–8 and to become downwardly mobile in terms of productivity, recognition, and power?

The example of Francis of Assisi is even more challenging. I am moved by Francis's radical emptying of himself, letting go totally of his privileged youth in dramatic gestures, like completely stripping himself in front of his father, bishop, and much of the town of Assisi and declaring that from then on, God would be his only "father." Tattered robes, a cave for a home, begging for food, working with lepers, trusting totally in God to provide what he needed — this was the "fare" Francis foresaw for any true follower of Jesus' Gospel. There is no way to imitate all the specifics of Francis's experiment with poverty, but we can experiment. And we can, and should, take on the spirit of Francis's poverty, even if its external manifestations are not entirely appropriate. I'll try to explain this in terms of love, humility, and joy, poverty's three special companions for Francis.

Francis's description of poverty was *vivere sine proprio* — "to live without possessions." Why? For love of God. To become one with God, to realize the Kingdom of God in ourselves, to experience that oneness that embraces all of reality, we must let go of everything else. In Gandhian terms, we must "reduce ourselves to zero" in order to realize All. Jesus' advice to the rich young man was "to sell all, give it to the poor, and come, follow me." In other words, get rid of everything that would hinder your commitment to me and follow me, love me, totally. I will lead you to everything. Love is the goal. Poverty is the way. It is "the gateway through which we pass into freedom *from* our egos, into the freedom *for* God," as two contemporary Franciscans put it. The original and truest Franciscan with Francis, his "soul sister" Clare, put it similarly: "This poverty, my beloved brothers and sisters, cling to with all your being, and *for the love of our Lord Jesus Christ* do not under any circumstances, want to possess anything" (italics mine).[32]

Vivere sine proprio — but, how do we live without possessions, especially in the interior senses of this injunction? In summary, the Gospel, as Francis understood it, asks us to renounce all earthly possessions, *everything that would give us security. We are to renounce all claims.* Yes, this does mean letting go of all earthly possessions. It does mean not using more than what I need to live a full human life. Perhaps I don't need to *own* everything, even anything. For example, we can use the public library for our reading needs. Even if we do own things, we can move in the direction of Paul's injunction, "whether I feast or fast, I do all for the love of Christ Jesus." Whether I have a car that works well or not, I'll use what I have for the love of God. I'll enjoy it, use it well while I have it, but should I lose it tomorrow, I won't fret, get bitter, stop my work. I won't let it affect my love of God and the ministry to which I am called. I'll simply take the bus or ask a friend for a ride. Francis probably had that kind of detachment or indifference in mind.

Beulah Caldwell, a Cherokee friend of our family, has shown us a similar attitude toward possessions characteristic of Native American peoples. Things are gifts in two senses. Besides being gifts of God to us, our things can become gifts of ourselves to others. Several times Beulah has gifted us with her best pottery. Admire a work of art in the home of many Native Americans and you may find yourself the recipient of that art. I recently had a brief debate with myself about how to distribute pictures from a special trip. Immediately I set aside the best ones for myself, parcelling out the left-overs for my friends. That act of possessiveness haunted me. Soon afterward I wanted to give two friends a thank-you gift. When I gave them the crucifix I brought back from Nicaragua, the crucifix became even more special to me, especially when I see it hanging in their home. Why do we keep the best for ourselves and give others our left-overs?

If I care too much about my possessions, I spend time worrying about them, protecting them from others. I try to serve two masters. Francis's insight into the relationship between property and violence, materialism and militarism, is amazingly contemporary. Speaking to the Bishop of Assisi, who had told Francis that his ideal of poverty was too difficult, Francis stated: "My Lord, if we had possessions, we should also need weapons for their protection. From that proceeds the contentions and quarrels that obstruct the love of God and humankind. For that reason we want to possess naught of the things of this world."

Raymond Hunthausen, Catholic archbishop of Seattle and a Franciscan in spirit, echoes Francis's words: "Nuclear arms protect privilege and exploitation. Giving them up would mean our having to give up economic power over other peoples. Peace and justice go together. On the path we now follow, our economic policies toward other countries require nuclear weapons. Giving up the weapons would mean giving up more than our means of global terror. It would mean giving up the reason for such terror — our privileged place in the world."

We are to let go of all security other than God — which Francis described as "renouncing all claims." And not just claims to property and money, but all claims — gender, position, age, experience, effort. I should not reject any persons, any tasks, because they are "beneath me." Each time I hear myself about to say, "men don't," "directors don't," or "your father doesn't," I need to resist this temptation to place myself above others, rather than at their service. Any time I am about to say "you owe me" (money, a favor, a wage, "consideration"), I should reflect first. Not that I cannot ask for and hope for a favor in return for all the favors I've done for that person, but I need to let go of any hint of demand that would hinder the other's free response. Francis says this is especially true in our relationship to God. God owes us nothing. All my good deeds do not merit me anything. "Salvation" — God's Kingdom of Shalom — is an entirely free gift. And that, says Francis, should be our stance toward everyone we encounter.

To renounce all claims — even to my time. It's not mine in the first place. How hard it is for me to face this! God gives me this day in order to love. I have an agenda of what I think this means in terms of all the responsibilities and people in my life. But should God see my day a little differently and send unexpected people and situations my way, I hope I'm "available." All this requires humility, poverty's second friend. Just as nothing is "beneath me," so too God's agenda for me may not be my original agenda. If it's not, then I had better make it mine. I am not the one in control. Jesus is Lord, not just of history, but of *my life and my "today."*

Poverty's third friend is joy. The haunting song from the movie *Brother Sun, Sister Moon* has this refrain: "If you want to live life free, take your time, go slowly. Do few things but do them well...." Another hard saying for someone like me who is so task-oriented. If I can make four calls in thirty minutes instead of just two or three, all the better. If I can plan a workshop at the same time as I am doing the dishes or even listening to one of my children describe a movie, why not? I eat quickly, write quickly, move quickly through almost every task I do. Have you ever found yourself saying "I'm eating on the run" or "I'll just grab a bite"? I know I don't slow down enough and savor or relish people, experiences, the goodness of creation. Even the words "savor" and "relish" have a wonderful sound to them. I need to savor many more moments in my day, even if only for

a few seconds. I think Francis was such a joyful person, even
in his poverty, because he savored the simple things of creation.
He savored his moments with people, with God. He savored
each morsel of food. He took nothing for granted. He wasn't
"satiated" in our materialistic sense. How many people caught
up in affluence are never satisfied — always more, newer, bigger,
better. And always the next project, all the items on my agenda
that keep me from enjoying what I am about at this moment.
Presence, simplicity, joy — they seem to go together.

Francis renounced all possessions, all earthly security, all
claims, because he belonged totally to God. He saw himself as a
visitor and pilgrim on earth and put this in his rule for Franciscans: "The brothers should acquire nothing as owners, neither a
house nor a foundation, nor any other thing. And just as 'pilgrims and strangers' (1 Peter 2:11) who in this world serve the
Lord in poverty and humility, they should with confidence ask
alms...." In the end we will have to let go of everything anyway
if we want to embrace God at the moment of death, so why not
prepare for that surrender in the present? And not just prepare
for it, but begin to live it in the present.

God's Kingdom of Shalom is to be lived in the present as
much as we can. In so doing, we offer ourselves as witnesses
of that Kingdom, as Francis and Franciscans have been doing for
eight centuries. Whether we like it or not, we are called to be
witnesses that God's Kingdom of Shalom is breaking out in the
world. It is possible to live it. The world needs desperately to
see it. Our journey is not a private affair. That doesn't make it
any easier, but it gives it more significance. I will struggle to be
faithful to what I think is my calling, so that your faith and hope
are increased. Isn't that what it means to be followers of Jesus?
Isn't that the "oneness of life" we are trying to embody?

Connecting with the Earth

Return to the beautiful hymn of Chief Seattle (p. 11 above),
where he instructs us non-Native American people: "Teach your
children what we have taught our children — that the earth is
our mother. Whatever befalls the earth befalls the children of
the earth.... This we know. The earth does not belong to us; we
belong to the earth."

Rural families as well as Native American communities have

much to teach us "city folks" about the message of the Scriptures embodied in passages such as: "The earth is the Lord's and the fullness thereof" (Ps. 24); "the land belongs to me, and to me you are only strangers and guests" (Lev. 25:23). We do not really own anything. We are *stewards* of the earth and of its rich variety of resources. In chapter 8 we will consider how to live as children of our mother earth, in solidarity with the earth.

Simplifying Our Lives

In our experiments with truth to simplify our lives, the process is more important than the product. There is no "right answer" that satisfies all households, congregations, situations. There are no quantitative measures of what constitutes a "simple lifestyle" or "Gospel living." There are some qualitative measures that are helpful, for example: "will this particular service, product, or location I am considering make me more compassionate or less compassionate, bring me closer to the poor or separate me further from the poor?" Gandhi's way of putting this question is dramatic: "Whenever you are in doubt or when the self becomes too much with you, try the following expedient: Recall the face of the poorest and most helpless person you have ever seen and ask yourself if the step you contemplate is going to be of any use to him.... Then you will find your doubts and your self melting away."

"Right answers" or "good answers" will *emerge* from a process that involves prayer, study, discussion, and action. Prayer readies our hearts to hear voices different from the prevailing societal voices and values, especially the voice of God in Scripture. God speaks to us through other prophets as well and their voices can help us on our journey.[33]*

The discernment necessary for raising the right questions and facing challenging answers involves other people. We need to place ourselves in relationship to people who challenge us by their fidelity and courage, who help us understand ourselves, and who can support us in difficult choices and actions. Whether from a spiritual director, a support group, or a trusted friend, outside feedback, challenge, and support are essential.

Third, the process involves mutuality, especially when a family or community is involved. Decisions that affect the whole household should involve all members of the household. Family actions on behalf of the poor or in defense of creation should be the result of family decisions. Regular family or community meetings that include "family service" or "community service" discussions and decisions regarding household purchases and other lifestyle issues are an important tool for involving all household members and making sure that the needs of everyone, children included, are taken seriously.

One family who convinced us early about the importance of family meetings described their negative experience this way: "Our teenage daughters became very upset with us one Saturday morning when we announced that we were going to buy a used sofa at a Goodwill store that day. They screamed, 'Mother, you are keeping us poor, we don't have to be poor, and we're embarrassed to bring our friends around this house!' My husband and I had made all those lifestyle decisions without the kids' input and continued to do so. Now our daughters are grown with families of their own, and they are pursuing lives of conspicuous consumption. If we could do it over again, we would definitely involve them in decisions."

Our own family experience of including our children (now teens) into most of our lifestyle decisions over the last ten years has strengthened our conviction about the family meeting process. We have made many compromises, but the children do not seem to resent our values and have internalized them to some extent. All of them, for instance, are still quite comfortable buying their clothes at second-hand stores, especially when they realize how this stretches their individual clothing budgets. Kathy and I make a clear distinction between nonnegotiable values and negotiable ways of living out those values. Concern for the poor, family service, recycling, more simple or less materialistic living are all nonnegotiable. But how much, how often, where, with whom are negotiable.

Finding Support

Living on Gospel terms depends heavily on the environment we create by our choices. For instance, where we choose to live (for those who have a choice) has a tremendous influence on our values and especially on the formation of our children's values. The choice of a home affects other choices: where we worship, shop, send our children to school, who their peers will be. If our environment is not conducive to the values we want to promote, then we have to take compensatory steps.

For example, if you live in a monocultural environment, you can compensate to some extent by the reading material and pictures you bring into your home.[34*] Worshipping, shopping, or enjoying cultural events in places that put you in touch with people of different racial, ethnic, or religious backgrounds promotes a more inclusive lifestyle. Such steps extend our sense of "oneness" across racial lines.

If you live in a relatively affluent environment, you can compensate to some extent by developing friendships with people from different economic backgrounds. Inviting an elderly poor person to dinner is often less threatening to our children or other reluctant members of our household than providing temporary shelter for a homeless person. Regular community service projects — like serving a meal at a soup kitchen, especially if mutual relationships are fostered; nursing home visits; an outing with residents from a shelter for the homeless — all these can put us in situations and with persons who can broaden our horizons, deepen our compassion, and enliven our faith.

Probably the most important way to support our (and our children's) values is through a family support group. When adults and children come together regularly for joint prayer, study, action, support, and fun, good things happen. Because living on Gospel terms ultimately means a conversion in our lives and a life-long commitment to solidarity with the poor that will lead us to experience the cross of Jesus, we all need the challenge and support of others over the long haul. Children especially need to be with children from other families with similar values. It is hard to be different.

Living on Gospel terms is difficult because Jesus asks us to come follow him, not to suburbia but to the cross. Living as lilies of the field — seeking security more and more in God and less in high-yield investments — is as scary as it is unclear. Can we let go and place that much trust in God's providential love for us? Choosing simplicity or even downward mobility is craziness in a society that exalts the beautiful, the rich, and the powerful, and constantly says that "more is better."

Lent is an especially appropriate time to wrestle with these questions and let Jesus take our hand and lead us another step along his journey through Calvary to the Resurrection. Here is the real "fullness of life," the genuinely "good life" that is God's Kingdom of Shalom. Do we dare to believe and to follow? We have God's promises to be with us always: "I will never forget you. See, I have carved you on the palm of My hand..." (Isa. 49:15); "you did not choose me; no, I chose you..." (John 15:16); "and know that I am with you always; yes, to the end of time" (Matt. 28:20).

For Reflection

1. What does it mean to "seek first the Kingdom of God" in decisions about jobs and careers, about spending money, about spending time, both individual time and family time?

2. What does "preferential option for the poor" mean concretely in your life?

3. How much trust does God want when we are asked to "consider the lilies of the field"? How much is "enough" for you when it comes to financial security, insurance policies?

4. What are ways you can incorporate hospitality more fully into your heart and home?

5. Jon Sobrino, a Jesuit theologian, peacemaker, and prophet from El Salvador, has described solidarity in these terms: "Solidarity means to conceive of life in such a way that we are really open to give the best we have to other people, and to be open to receive from other people."[35] Recalling the example of Beulah Caldwell's gift giving, how are you already "giving your best to others"? Are there ways you could experiment with giving more of your best? I have to examine myself continuously on how I distribute my "best time." Do Kathy and the children get only my left-overs — when I am too tired to work?

6. Are you happy with where you live? In what ways yes and what ways no? What can you do to bring your living situation more into line with what you truly value?

7. Is there more you can do to involve other members of your household in your "experiments with truth" in lifestyle and make them more of a family affair or community effort?

8. Is there more you can do to improve the support systems you and your household need for living on Gospel terms rather than on materialistic terms?

Chapter 7

Love Is the Measure

I HAVE PROBABLY HEARD THE THIRTEENTH CHAPTER of Paul's first letter to the Corinthians at least fifty times. I know that "the greatest of these is charity," that any prophetic utterance without love is like "sounding brass and tinkling cymbals." But it wasn't until a couple of years ago that this truth began to really penetrate my heart. It began in the midst of a period of real depression in my life, when I had lost much of my confidence and joy and sense of the future. In the midst of that uncertainty, I read Jim Forest's biography of Dorothy Day entitled *Love Is the Measure*. The witness of her life hit me hard, calling into question not so much what I had been doing, but how I had been doing it. Was the measure of my life love, or was it accomplishment, completing tasks, being productive? Unfortunately in my case the measure has generally been the latter.

Since that moment I have been on a journey into compassion as the inner core of what it means to be a peacemaker, prophet, and disciple. In his meditative book on St. Francis, Carlo Carretto writes: "Out beyond the confines of my self, by His pure gift of Himself, I had entered into the life of the true mystery which ruled the invisible universe, and I had clutched, as only a poor person can, the revelation of true love. *What counted in life was not to do, but to love.* What saved the world was not our wisdom, and not our action: *it was the power of the love of God, lived in each one of us.* On the human level, Christ's life was a failure. But on the level of His love, it was the masterpiece that gave new life to all creation. By dying for love, Christ had exalted the whole world. Death had been vanquished."[36]

This was the power of Jesus, his unconditional love, *agape*, the love of God operating in the human heart. Nonviolence as "the power that manifests itself in us when we become aware of the oneness of life," in Gandhi's definition, means precisely love. Because he so embodied an acute awareness of his oneness with

75

all persons and with creation itself, Gandhi radiated a power that
was able to touch even his stiffest opponents. Eventually many
of them became convinced of Gandhi's sincere love for them, his
appreciation of their situation, and his willingness to work for
their well-being.

This love is confirmed by the peacemaker's willingness to
suffer rather than inflict suffering. It was in Jesus' acceptance
of death and his forgiveness of those who killed him ("Father,
forgive them for they know not what they do") that we are convinced of his love and God's love for us. It was in the giving
of their lives for others that King, Gandhi, Francis, Dorothy Day,
Mother Teresa, Jean Donovan, and countless others have discovered the power of love, the power to touch people, the power
to transform hearts and structures. We have considered several
ways of developing and deepening this power of nonviolent, suffering love for all creation — prayer, fasting, simplifying our life-
styles. In this chapter, we will look at one-to-one peacemaking
and side-by-side service as ways to become more aware of the
oneness of life.

One-to-One Peacemaking
with Our Nearest and Dearest

Affirmation

Perhaps the most difficult, and the best, place to practice unconditional love is with the people to whom we are closest —
those we live with, those we work with. We see the faults and
failings in our loved ones so much more than their strengths and
good points. We are often more critical of family members than
of anyone else. When I look at a report card with three "B's"
and three "C's," I invariably comment on the "C's" first, unless
I catch myself. I tolerate behaviors at work that I do not tolerate
at home. I once heard a man describe his face as a "No face" —
a face that said no to his family, co-workers, and everyone else.
He was trying to develop a "Yes face." I realized that my face
probably said no much more than yes, and that I wore my "No
face" at home more than anywhere else. I have been trying to
wear my "Yes face" more often. For some, smiling does not come
easy. But how comfortable and affirmed we feel in the presence
of someone who smiles. A smile is the fruit of a centered, loving heart, but it can also nurture such a heart. A good place to

start our "experiments with truth" in one-to-one peacemaking is
a smiling "Yes face."

Nonviolence of the Tongue

Another area for experimentation is with our words. The past
several months I have been playing a beautiful cassette tape,
Teaching Peace, as part of my peacemaking workshops with children and families. The refrain of one of the songs goes like this:

> I think you're wonderful;
> when someone says that to me,
> it makes me feel wonderful,
> as wonderful can be.
> It makes me want to say
> the same thing to somebody new —
> "And by the way,
> I've been meaning to say,
> I think you're wonderful too."[37]

As I sing it with groups, I can see in their eyes how true these
lyrics are. Then I found myself thinking about my own home,
especially in the morning as everyone is rushing off to school
and work. When was the last time I sent any of them off feeling
wonderful? The first time I asked myself that question, I was
ashamed of my answer and it brought tears to my eyes. But that
realization also brought me to decision and conversion. And this
morning at least one of my children got a big hug as she was
racing out the door.

Attentiveness to Others

A third step in one-to-one peacemaking is becoming more
aware of and responsive to the feelings and needs of others —
attentiveness to others. The more wrapped up in ourselves we
are, the more difficult it is to focus on others, to hear their needs,
to sense their feelings. The more preoccupied we are with our
agenda, whether it is work projects, deadlines, things we covet,
our feelings and needs, the less we are attentive to others. There
have to be spaces in our day when we can slow down, drop our
own agendas, maybe even get in touch with our own feelings
and needs for the first time, and be truly present to those around

us. The more centered a person I am, that is, the more I take time
to be still and get rid of the many distractions that keep me un-
centered, the more I can be present and sensitive to others and
really hear them. The Catholic bishops at the Second Vatican
Council began their insightful document *The Church in the Mod-
ern World* with the following description of human compassion,
which can apply to our one-to-one peacemaking as well. They
spoke directly to Christians but their words could be extended
to people of all faiths: "The joys and the hopes, the griefs and
the anxieties of the people of this age, especially those who are
poor or in any way afflicted, these too are the joys and hopes, the
griefs and anxieties of the followers of Christ. Indeed, nothing
genuinely human fails to raise an echo in their hearts" (no. 1).

I am learning this attentiveness in a special way in the nursing homes I visit every two weeks, trying to be present to each
person I visit, knowing that I don't have a quota or rigid schedule that keeps me moving from room to room. Kathy has helped
me see the wisdom of allowing a few more minutes for chores,
getting ready to go out with the kids, trips to the store, phone
calls — to avoid that last-minute rushing that increases tension
and irritation and prohibits relaxed conversation. I have a long
way to go, but the initial experiments are bearing fruit. Is this an
area where you need to experiment too? Where is a good place
to start?

Reconciliation

We've already looked at the need to take unilateral initiatives
in reaching out to our "opponents." Whether this is saying "I'm
sorry" first, or doing a favor for someone, the intention is the
same and so generally is the effect. The walls of hostility, the
barriers between us (Eph. 2:13–16), begin to crumble and God's
Kingdom of Shalom becomes more a reality.

Little surprises for people are another way of telling them they
are wonderful. Thoughtful surprises are a superb instrument of
reconciliation, a way of practicing attentiveness and of taking the
focus off myself, a way to encourage my "Yes face" to come out
more often. Doing little favors, especially when people feel sad
or burdened, makes me a more compassionate person — and a
more effective peacemaker and prophet. This is not to suggest
that we swallow injustices or hurts silently. It's important to say

how we feel and what we think needs to be changed. But it is equally important to get past the hurts and work for reconciliation. Eliminating or at least reducing our desire to retaliate in interpersonal conflicts is essential. Reaching out to persons I am struggling with by doing a tiny chore for them, offering a ride instead of telling them to walk, or putting a note in their lunch bag or mail slot all have a way of reducing the tension and increasing the prospects for reconciliation. It's a way of telling your "opponents" that you are not out to get them. They can relax a little, let down their guard, and take a chance too in working out the conflict.

Hospitality

Opening our home to others is a way of opening our hearts, whether those others are neighbors, our children's friends, out-of-town visitors, teens or homeless people in need of temporary shelter, aging relatives. Making ourselves and our possessions available, especially that ultimate possession, our home, transforms our hearts little by little.

An integral part of Gandhi's nonviolence was his "ashrams." These were places where his followers — "satyagrahis" — were "formed." These houses of formation were his "laboratories of love" in which his followers lived a community life in service to one another and to the community around them. Nonviolence, for Gandhi, was a holistic way of life, not merely a strategy for social change. Its effectiveness as a strategy was contingent, in Gandhi's mind, on a significant number of its practitioners living out the full implications of nonviolence as a way of life.

One-to-One Peacemaking with Strangers — "Benevolent Glancing"

A marvelous way to practice compassion is what Mary Evelyn Jegen has called "benevolent glancing." Like many others, I have been captivated by her simple suggestion:

A small news item about Pope John Paul's visit to Southeast Asia a few years ago turned out to be a powerful impulse in my ongoing effort to integrate prayer and ways of working for peace. The news item told about the pope's visit to the supreme patriarch of the Buddhists of Thailand. Protocol for that visit required that the two men sit together for a half hour in absolute silence while they "exchanged benevolent glances." Not long after I read the story, I decided to give benevolent glancing a try. At first I felt a bit awkward. However, I was protected by my anonymity, since I was making this first experiment on a Chicago bus. I did not try to engage anyone's eyes, so in effect the benevolent glancing was strictly a unilateral initiative. A strange thing happened. I found I was praying — not saying prayers, but being attentive, alert, and aware in a way impossible to describe. For whatever reason, I wanted to look on the other with love. And love is what benevolence is all about, since the word itself means "to wish another well."

What has all this to do with peace? Benevolent glancing is the art of attentiveness. Paying attention to what is before us is a way of prayer. It is almost a definition of prayer.... Benevolent glancing is relishing God by directly attending to what is immediately before us.... Peacemaking and contemplation are so intimately related that one can hardly exist without the other. This truth can be appreciated by recognizing that violence depends on distorting the object or the victim of violence, turning the victim into an impersonal object which can then be injured or even killed....

To try benevolent glancing is to experience deeply stirred emotions, ranging from embarrassment to fear, to compassion, and almost inevitably to love. Fear of invading a person's privacy causes the embarrassment, but this initial feeling can be shaped into what we traditionally call modesty, a way of respect, reverence, even awe in the presence of the splendor of the human person who is "little less than the angels ... crowned with glory and honor" (Psalm 8).[38]

I have experimented with benevolent glancing off and on for two years, in a variety of situations, and I am convinced of its benefits. I do a lot of walking and it is at these times that I experiment the most. I have learned that it is easier for me to add a verbal greeting to the greeting of my eyes. People seem less uncomfortable and more responsive to a "good morning" accompanying my smile. I often think of Murray Bodo's account of Francis and how he loved people with his eyes. And I think of all the years that my face has not loved, has said no, and kept people at a distance.

Another place where my experiments are most vital are the streets downtown that I walk as "Francis the Clown," on my way to and from the shelters I visit. I am very aware of the need all persons have to be recognized and treated with respect. People living on the street or in shelters are so beaten down, generally have such low regard for themselves because few people have any regard for them, that I feel a special calling to affirm their dignity as persons. In part I do this with my eyes. But I also like to make a fuss over them and give them a Hershey "kiss."

"In India," writes Ram Dass, "when we meet and part we often say, 'Namaste,' which means: I honor the place in you where the entire universe resides; I honor the place in you of love, of light, of truth, of peace. I honor the place within you where if you are in that place in you and I am in that place in me, there is only one of us."[39]

Add the traditional Hindu gesture of folded hands and bow and you have as sacred a gesture of affirmation and love as I can conceive. I long to use that gesture, to share its richness, with others, as I do in workshops and at this moment in this book. And as I am learning from Francis the Clown, you don't have to put on the make-up and dress of a clown to affirm people's dignity, especially those people whose dignity is denied them daily in so many ways. In the process, watch what happens to your heart. You will become a more compassionate person, I guarantee. If it can happen to me, a master of productive, scheduled behavior, it can happen to anyone.

An old Hasidic tale answers the question "How do we know when dawn is near?" this way: "It is when you can look into the face of the Others and recognize them as our brothers and sisters. Until then, it is night." Dare we hope that dawn is near? We can be instruments of that dawning, instruments of God's compassion in the world. But we must yield to that incredible calling, risk feeling foolish as we experiment with initiatives like benevolent glancing. Not everyone responds positively, but we will plant seeds or nurture seeds already planted, and we will transform our own hearts.

Henri Nouwen's insight into the links between contemplation and ministry is pertinent here as we reflect on the place of service in our lives: "What more beautiful ministry is there than the ministry by which we make others aware of the love, truth, and beauty they reveal to us."[40] To recognize "that of God" in each person and then to affirm and call forth that goodness has long been my understanding of ministry. It is not so much what we "do for" people, but what we "do with" them, calling forth their unique gifts. When we serve people in nursing homes, class-rooms, shelters, our goal should be to help them feel less needy, more gifted, and more able to share their gifts. Traditional "help-ing" relationships need to become as reciprocal as possible.

Side-by-Side Service

Side-by-side compassionate service of others who are hurting was, for Gandhi, an essential part of his formation program for "satyagrahis." The importance of this dimension of disciple-ship has been brought home to me whenever I ask people to identify those experiences that have nurtured their compassion and courage. Invariably they cite encounters with human suf-fering. Gandhi's major national campaigns of nonviolent non-cooperation in India were in 1920–22, 1930–32, and 1940–42. During the intervening time, while he spent much of it in jail, he had his "satyagrahis" living in some of India's 700,000 vil-lages, engaged in what he called his "Constructive Programme." This was essentially working side-by-side with the rural poor of India, promoting village and human development. Nothing was beneath the dignity of "satyagrahis," particularly the work of the "Untouchables." If Gandhi was going to eradicate the scourge of untouchability from India, it had to be first eradicated from the hearts of those who professed nonviolence.

The caste system in India was very influential in determining attitudes and behavior (and it still is, to some extent; I experi-enced in 1972 its remnants even among those who called them-selves Gandhians). And I can identify traces of elitism in myself. Gandhi felt those who wanted to practice nonviolence as a way of life had to learn to live side-by-side with the poor, how to love them and be loved by them, how to empower them and be empowered by them, how to struggle against poverty. This ex-perience would transform their hearts to become more effective instruments in God's transformation of society.

Going to the villages was much more a spiritual journey into self-emptying love for Gandhi than a physical journey into rural India. Jim Douglass writes: "Satyagrahis must serve the people by helping to rekindle the fire under the ashes, the divine power of liberation within their suffering. By extinguishing their own desire for power, the satyagrahis seek the authentic power of the people. They must discover in contemplation, and in the giving of their lives, those symbolic actions which will ignite the people's faith to resist injustice with their whole lives, lives coming together as a united force of truth and thus releasing the liberating power of the God within them."[41] Practitioners of nonviolence have to be compassionate persons above all. Otherwise, as Paul tells us, we're nothing more than "sounding brass and tinkling cymbals."

In the movie *Gandhi* there is a scene at the Moslem leader Jinnah's palatial home, where Gandhi, Jinnah, Nehru, Patel, and several others are discussing strategy. Gandhi suggests a national day of prayer and fasting, which would mean a nationwide work stoppage that the British couldn't defeat in propaganda terms because of its religious character. In the course of the discussion, a servant enters the room with a service of tea on an ornate silver tray. Gandhi immediately takes the tray and begins to serve the others, to the consternation of both the servant and the other Indian leaders. Gandhi acknowledges that he did it deliberately to demonstrate to them how they had to be transformed as much as the country. We are often in similar positions and can practice serving others — clearing dishes after a meal, offering to pour the coffee, volunteering to get the snacks while watching TV with others, washing out the coffee mugs at the office, helping with a task that another normally does alone. The possibilities are almost limitless. The results are the same — a more caring, compassionate heart.

There is a scene in various depictions of the life of Francis where, as a young pilgrim, he encounters a leper.[42] Francis says he had always avoided lepers; he dreaded the thought of meeting them. Here he is, face to face with a leper and no one else around. Instead of fleeing in disgust, he embraces the leper, kisses his physically repugnant face, and is transformed in the process. That moment of conversion marked the beginning of Francis's willingness to embrace the poor, to do side-by-side service with lepers and others, and thereby to develop the com-

passionate heart that made him the effective peacemaker he has
been over the last eight centuries.

As I reflect on both Gandhi and Francis, I see first the faces of
the people at the nursing homes who have tubes in their noses,
who smell, who are in no way "beautiful" in the world's terms,
but to whom I am almost irresistibly drawn, once I got past my
initial revulsions. Now my hands want to reach out to touch
them, bless them, even though they are generally not even aware
of my presence at their bedside. I recall scenes of Mother Teresa
walking from bed to bed in her home for the dying in Calcutta.
She touches the foreheads of each person in a blessing. Slow is
her gait, compassionate her touch. There's power in her hands.
I know the power that radiates from my own hands in the nursing home. You probably have experienced this same power of
compassionate touch with children, with the elderly, or with others.

Gandhi had a profound insight for educators: what the hands
do, the heart will learn. The hands are the instrument of insight,
the channel through which insight comes. That's why he stressed
spinning for all Indians, especially for "satyagrahis." That's why
manual labor was essential in his ashrams and in the schools
organized in India along Gandhian principles. There are no cooks
and janitors in Gandhian schools; students do their own cooking
and cleaning. There are also vegetable gardens and opportunities
for direct service. Gandhi's educational philosophy and practice
focused equally on the head, the heart, and the hands. If one is
missing, then the whole person is not being educated, nor will
society be transformed.

Moksha in Hindu thought is the ultimate achievement of freedom from the cycle of births and deaths. Its generally other-
worldly interpretation as detachment from action was rejected
by Gandhi in favor of detachment from one's ego and total surrender to God through service to and union with all humanity.
In Gandhi's words: "For me the road to salvation lies through
incessant toil in the service of my country and thereby of humanity. I want to identify myself with everything that lives. In
the language of the *Gita,* I want to live at peace with both friend
and foe.... So my patriotism is for me a stage in my journey to
the land of eternal freedom and peace. Thus it will be seen that
for me there are no politics devoid of religion."[43]

Gandhi transformed the understanding of *moksha* and *yajna* (sacrifice) from a worship of God apart from God's universe, to a sacrifice of oneself for the sake of humanity. Our ultimate aim is the realization of God. But "the immediate service of all human beings becomes a necessary part of this endeavor simply because the only way to find God is to see God in God's creation and be one with it. This can only be done by service of all."[44] Thus it is only when we lose ourselves in the service of others that we attain self-realization, *moksha*, and true freedom. "God demands nothing less than complete self-surrender as the price for the only real freedom that is worth having."[45]

Extended Service Through "Material and Physical Accompaniment"

While most direct service opportunities in our lives are those in our own community, places and people we can visit regularly and develop mutual relationships that have a special way of touching our hearts and mobilizing our efforts, there are more distant possibilities that can stretch our hearts as well. In order to nurture our sense of solidarity with the whole of humanity and all parts of the earth, it is important to relate compassionately to human needs outside our own area.

Material Aid

Material aid is the option we are most familiar with. I've already mentioned this as part of a lifestyle of solidarity, sharing the savings we realize from sacrificial eating and other experiments in living on less. Our churches as well as peace and justice groups are always in the midst of relief efforts to victims of famine (as in Africa), of weather or war (as in Quest for Peace's aid to the people of Nicaragua[46]), of repression (as in SHARE's interfaith effort to help Salvadoran refugees going home to their former communities from Honduran refugee camps[47]).

The importance of such efforts is clear from "A Letter from Chalatenango: 'Return and Bring Us Food,'" written by Christians in El Salvador to people of faith in North America, through the *Letter to the Churches* biweekly publication of CRISPAZ (Cristianos por la Paz en El Salvador):

Dear Brothers and Sisters:

From the territories of our people, we Christians who live, suffer, and struggle here send you our affectionate greetings.

When you came to visit us, you came to know our situation, our desire to live in peace, our struggle to produce and obtain everything necessary to live in freedom and justice. You realized that all this effort we carried out with joy, and we did so willingly. With all our energy we set about the reconstruction of our communities after each military operation that the regime launches against these territories.

Now, a few months after your visit, we are in a difficult situation as a result of a new criminal action by the Army. On March 5, the Army began an operation in the same places you came to know, as well as the rest of eastern Chalatenango. Several hundred Christians with whom you shared your stay were taken out of their homes. All of us who were able to escape were left with nothing. The officials and the soldiers destroyed everything we had: basic grains, fields, houses, utensils, clothes and all.

Now we find ourselves with great difficulty to feed and clothe ourselves. For more than thirty days the government soldiers destroyed our places of shelter and work, persecuting the civilian population. You who came to know of our firm resolution to live here can imagine all the suffering we feel in being forced to abandon our homes and live in a refugee camp. We don't want to live in refugee camps nor live off charity. We have sufficient energy and an infinite vocation for freedom. We want to live and work in our communities.

This time we address ourselves to everyone, and especially to you — nourished by the affection that you showed us and by the hope that dwells in our hearts from your words — and we ask you to make every effort that you can to bring us food, clothing, and shoes. We are more than 400 families who are in need of food, as well as fertilizer, insecticide, and seeds for our crops.

We ask all of you to come to these areas to help us. Your visits comfort us.

Christian Communities of Chalatenango
April 29, 1986[48]*

When we find ourselves addressed as "brothers and sisters" and realize the human consequences of government policy, we want to respond.

As the letter indicates, our material aid can promote a deeper sense of solidarity when we make direct contact with the recipients of our "material accompaniment." Many congregations have formed partnerships with congregations or missions in the Third World. Often such partnerships involve correspondence between the two groups and sometimes between individuals and families within each group. "Sister City" projects provide similar opportunities for personal contact. Some people have made contact on their own, getting names from the mission agencies of their denominations or even reading mission magazines like *Maryknoll*.[49] Our Parenting for Peace and Justice Network has been promoting partnership relationships between family support groups in North America and their counterparts in the Third World and the U.S.S.R.

Physical Accompaniment

A more intense form of extended service is through what some call "physical accompaniment." During the 1980s, thousands of North Americans physically accompanied the people of Nicaragua as they suffered through a war largely due to U.S. policy. As one who was privileged to be part of this Witness for Peace effort, I know that the lives of every one of these North Americans will never be the same. It is an incredible experience of solidarity to walk with people in the midst of their struggle. Other "internationals" have accompanied the groups of refugees going home to El Salvador.

Standing in Solidarity

But we don't have to go overseas to physically accompany the victims of violence, injustice, and repression. There are such groups and individuals in our own communities as well. In some cases they are people of color. Sometimes they are the economically poor, sometimes people in prison or just released from prison. The mentally disabled are often discriminated against; no one wants a "group home" in their neighborhood. Perhaps more than any other group, gay and lesbian members of our communities (sometimes even in our congregations) are discriminated against to the point of being denied employment and housing, and, worse, are often the victims of violence and obscene hate campaigns. The spread of AIDS seems to have increased this violence instead of mobilizing public sympathy and action, as other health emergencies would. This is a difficult issue for many people and congregations to deal with, but if we don't stand in solidarity with the victims of gross violence and discrimination, how can we call ourselves disciples of Jesus? "Whatever you do to the least of my brothers and sisters, you do to me" (Matt. 25:40, 45).

"Standing in solidarity" can take many forms. A letter to the editor of our local newspaper in support of victims of discrimination or violence is one form of going public. Challenging racist, sexist, hateful jokes or comments takes courage but is part of standing in solidarity. Publicly defending the rights and promoting means of meeting the needs of such groups and individuals in church, school, or community gatherings also takes courage, but if we don't stand up for "the least of these," who will? Sometimes we can even join them in their actions — public demonstrations, delegations to visit church, political, or business leaders. These external actions are important, but equally important is the internal change that takes place. Taking time to listen to their stories and getting to know them as persons enriches the experience and contributes to our ongoing conversion toward becoming more compassionate and courageous disciples.

Lest all this overwhelm us, recall Jesus' breaking into the lives of his disciples huddled in fear in that upper room right after his crucifixion. He comes to us in the same way, knowing our weaknesses and failures to follow him, especially when the going gets rough. He sweat blood through his own struggle to accept God's will and can empathize with us. Jesus accepts us as we are, forgives our sinfulness, and sends us forth with a promise to walk with us every moment, every step along the way.

Is it worth all the effort, all the risk? After all, this is threatening. It sounds like "laying our lives on the line" or "laying down our lives." That's not easy, I know. What does Jesus promise his disciples if we dare to follow him? Listen to Jesus' reply to Peter's question: "What about us? We have left everything and followed you. What are we to have, then?" Jesus said to him, "I tell you solemnly, when all is made new and the Son of Man sits on his throne of glory, you will yourselves sit on twelve thrones to judge the twelve tribes of Israel. And everyone who has left houses, brothers, sisters, father, mother, children or land for the sake of my name will be repaid a hundred times over, and also inherit eternal life" (Matt. 19:27–30).

God also promises to hear the cry of the poor, a theme repeated over and over in the Psalms (see Pss. 72, 89, 91, 107, 113) and proclaimed in Mary's "Magnificat." We can stand with the victims of violence and injustice with confidence. Not that it will always work out the way we hope (recall Allan Boesak's words on the people of Mogopa in South Africa). But as the poor themselves witness to us, we have God's promise to empower us to fidelity in the struggle.

For Reflection

1. In the area of "one-to-one peacemaking with our nearest and dearest," are there steps you feel you could and should take?

2. What did you think about the idea of "benevolent glancing"? Are you at a point that you want to give it a try? If so, where is a good place to start?

3. Read prayerfully Jesus' own words on service (for example, Matt. 10:24ff. and 20:26–28) and Paul's hymn of praise to Jesus who humbled himself in service to all, even to accepting death on a cross (Phil. 2:6–8). Identify ways in which service is already a part of your life. You are probably compassionately present to many hurting people, though not always as fully and faithfully as you would like. Is there more you want to do?

4. Have there been times when you have stood in solidarity with others? Have there been times when you could have but didn't? Is there something you could do about that now? Are there situations coming up where your voice could be helpful on behalf of victims of violence or discrimination?

5. It's not the quantity of our actions, but the quality of love we bring to what we can realistically do. Consider again Carlo Carretto's words: "What counted in life was not to do, but to love. What saved the world was not our wisdom, and not our action: it was the power of the love of God, lived in each one of us." Gandhi, Dorothy Day, Francis, and others never thought love could be expressed apart from action, but it's the quality of the action that is crucial. "Love is the measure."

Chapter 8

Reconciliation with the Earth

I REGULARLY TAKE AN EARLY MORNING WALK with our dog, B.J. I keep him on a leash until we reach the park, where I let him experience a bit of unbridled freedom, running, chasing squirrels. Today, because of light rain, I kept him on his leash and walked around the block. Halfway through the walk, I realized that instead of my controlling him, pulling him along or back to keep in step with my pace, I ought to be yielding to his pace and be willing to pause at every third tree or so. I ought to let go of my need to control him (and everything else in my life) and let him lead me. It became clear in that moment how I was to write today — yielding to God's Spirit and not adhering to my own timetable of a chapter a day. Does it matter if today's chapter takes longer? We will become prophetic disciples and peacemakers only if we learn to yield to God's movement and will in our lives. If we are to be prophets, persons who speak for God, as "echoes" or "melodies" of God, then we must attune ourselves to that divine rhythm in our lives.

As I was drying his paws wet with the morning rain (so he wouldn't soil by favorite chair and his favorite sleeping place), I felt a special bond with B.J., and I recalled a similar bond with Ashes, the dog who accompanied me on my hermitage retreat in the mountains of New Mexico fifteen months earlier. Never before had I developed a real companionship with an animal. I was as far from a "pet lover" as a person could be. I was always the family member who blocked any suggestion of animals, of any kind, in the house. But in the mountains of New Mexico, alone with creation and with the Creator for a week, I fell in love. I already loved the mountains, but that week I feel in love with animals, through the companionship of Ashes. At one point hours before dawn, I even invited him into my little hut, to share the embers of a warm fire, instead of freezing in the mountain cold outside as he had the previous nights. I felt a special oneness, not only with Ashes, but with all of creation in those moments. That feeling returned this morning.

Urgency of the Issue

The oneness that is God's Kingdom of Shalom is a oneness with God and with the totality of God's creation, not just with the whole human family. The oneness of life, the awareness of which Gandhi described as the source of the power of nonviolence, is a solidarity that embraces the earth itself. I find it helpful to think of the earth in human and relational terms, as Chief Seattle and other native peoples do. Recall his eloquence about "Mother Earth": "Teach your children what we have taught our children — that the earth is our mother. Whatever befalls the earth, befalls the children of the earth. . . . This we know. The earth does not belong to us; we belong to the earth."

Francis has been called the patron saint of ecology, because of his tremendous love of the earth. He speaks of creation in personal and relational terms, of "brother sun" and "sister moon," "brother wind" and "sister air," "brother fire" and "mother earth." When we refuse to think of creation in personal terms and treat it as an object, we find ourselves exploiting creation. The earth becomes something you can buy and sell, like bright beads. Chief Luther Standing Bear of the Lakota Sioux nation put it this way: "Lack of respect for growing living things soon leads to lack of respect for humans too."[50]

The violation of people is paralleled by the violation of the earth itself. Both are victims of rape. The human species plunders the earth, our mother, as we plunder one another. Nations and peoples with high levels of violence tend to be nations and peoples who disregard the earth. Nonviolent societies and peoples tend to live more in harmony with nature. Those of us who live in the United States, and to some extent most other First World nations, have a lot of reconciling to do with the earth as well as with the sisters and brothers of our human species. We are clearly the readership Carlo Carretto had in mind when he had Francis say:

> Nonviolence is broader than [leaving people in peace]. Nonviolence regards first of all nature, the skies, the seas, the mines, the forests, the air, water, the home. These are the

first objects of nonviolence. It is a terrible sin you have committed all around you, and I do not know whether or not you
can still be saved. You have violated the forests, defiled the
seas, plundered everything like a bunch of bandits. If there
were a court of the skies, or of the seas..., all of you (or
almost all) would be under sentence of death. And perhaps
there is such a court. An invisible one. For your punishment
has certainly begun. You can scarcely breathe your air. Your
food has become unhealthy. Cancer assaults you with more
and more regularity. And now that you have destroyed nearly
everything, you have appointed me patron saint of ecology.
You have to admit, it is a little late....[51]

Carlo Carretto and Francis have not overstated their case. We
all have friends battling cancer. Our beloved beaches are being spoiled almost everywhere. Our forests and wilderness areas
are disappearing at an alarming rate, as are whole species by
the thousands. The violations are almost endless, but so are the
possibilities for action. The need for such reconciling actions is
urgent.

Our Response

The first step in reconciling ourselves with the earth has already
been suggested — begin to think of the earth in relational terms.
In speaking of land, naturalist Aldo Leopold put it insightfully:
"We abuse land because we regard it as a commodity belonging
to us. When we see land as a community to which we belong,
we may begin to use it with love and respect."[52]

"...Land as a community to which we belong," "brother sun
and sister moon," the earth as a person or community that can
speak to us, that can reveal to us who we truly are and who our
Creator is. As Steve Van Matre expressed it:

Yes, the earth speaks, but only to those who can hear with
their hearts. It speaks in a thousand, thousand small ways,
but like our lovers and families and friends, it often sends its
messages without words. For you see, the earth speaks in the
language of love. Its voice is in the shape of a new leaf, the
feel of a water-worn stone, the color of evening sky, the smell
of summer rain, the sound of the night wind. The earth's

whispers are everywhere, but only those who have slept with it can respond readily to its call. . . .

Come, listen to the earth with us. For earth lovers, the natural world remains an inexhaustible source of delight: the sounds, textures, colors, shapes, patterns, harmonies; the sensate joy, the enchantment, the endless surprises. Earth lovers know that no man-made setting can ever hope to attain the richness, the drama, the meaning found in most any patch of wild land. Like a bottomless well in our oasis in space, the wonders of the earth can be drawn upon to recharge the spirit for all of one's days. Be an earth lover. Sleep with the earth. It will teach thee.[53]

My love relationship with the earth has taken on added depth in the past two years, since that mountain top experience in New Mexico. I came off that mountain understanding why I had chosen the name "Francis" for my clown character. I had discovered Francis of Assisi for the first time in my life and had fallen in love with him and with all those whom he loved — God, the poor, the whole of creation.

As "Francis the Clown" I began my experiments with the truth of Francis's life. One of the first areas of experimentation was in deepening my love of the earth. At some point early in the process, the following expression of this love crystallized and has served as the basis of my ongoing experimentation and the teaching I do about loving the earth. "See the earth with love in your eyes. Touch the earth with love in your hands. Walk the earth with love in your feet." I have also added at times, "Listen to the earth with love in your ears," recalling Steve Van Matre's experience that the earth does speak to us, if we have the hearts to listen.

"See the Earth with Love in Your Eyes"

To really see, we need to be really present, attentive to what is around us, not preoccupied or self-centered. I have to slow down, let go, and focus. Sometimes by placing myself in conducive environments and equipping myself with a camera to help my eyes see more sharply, I see more. And not just see more things, but I see them with a clarity and depth that I would not have otherwise experienced. Sunrise is a special moment of sight and insight for me. It became even more special a year ago when I discovered Byrd Baylor's magnificent hymn to the sun:

> The way to start a day is this — go outside and face the east and greet the sun with some kind of blessing or chant or song that you made yourself and keep for early morning. The way to make the song is this — don't try to think what words to use until you're standing there alone. When you feel the sun, you'll feel the song, too. Just sing it.... A morning needs to be sung to. A new day needs to be honored. People have always known that. Didn't they chant at dawn in the sun temples of Peru?... Didn't the pharaohs of Egypt say the only sound at dawn should be the sound of songs that please the morning sun? They knew what songs to sing. People always seemed to know.... And everywhere they knew to turn their faces eastward as the sun came up. Some people still know. When the first pale streak of light cuts through the darkness, wherever they are, those people make offerings and send mysterious strong songs to the sun. They know exactly how to start a day....
>
> Some people say there is a new sun every day, that it begins its life at dawn and lives for one day only. They say you have to welcome it. You have to make the sun happy. You have to make a good day for it. You have to make a good world for it to live its one-day life in. And the way to start, they say, is just by looking east at dawn. When they look east tomorrow, you can too. Your song will be an offering — and you'll be one more person in one more place at one more time in the world saying hello to the sun, letting it know you are there. If the sky turns a color sky never was before, just watch it. That's part of the magic. That's the way to start a day.[54]

When I begin my day with such a special moment of sight, especially when I combine that sight with hymns of gratitude and praise, my whole day is affected. My whole day tends to become more insightful, thankful, an act of praise, a prayer in its fullest sense. I am more gentle, present to those immediately around me, and aware of the oneness of life, especially my connectedness with the earth and all those celebrating the earth around the world, as Baylor's hymn proclaims.

She adds singing to seeing. I can attest to the mutual enrichment of that combination. Recalling the image of our true self as a melody of God, let's give in to that "temptation" to break out (at least softly) in song, especially when we are in the midst of the beauty of God's creation. Learning to play a musical instrument can be a major effort, but I know how important my guitar and recorder have been in different periods of my life in helping me see and savor the beauty around me. Music has given my poetry another expression enabling me to become more a melody myself.

I have enjoyed the times when I enriched my sight with photography. Not only did the camera help me see more at the moment of focus, but the pictures have provided rich capsules of insight. My journaling the past few years has been photojournaling. I combine my reflections with my pictures whenever possible. My first creation as "Francis the Clown" was my *Love the Earth* book in which I combined my own poetic expressions of love for the earth with those of others and pictures of my lover in her various poses. The combination becomes a fuller revelation. At some point in your next week, month, or year, consider taking a "sabbatical" and produce your own *Love the Earth* book. It's not hard. Put it in a three-hole folder or binder, so that you can continue to develop the book. Expressing our love deepens our love.

Mountain tops are a special place for seeing. I have been to the top of many mountains, on several continents, but the moment I remember most was 12,000 feet up on the Altiplano in the Peruvian Andes, overlooking the village of Camacani and expansive Lake Titicaca:

> I went to the top of the earth
>   to come down to earth,
> to discover the earth —
>   the shades and textures of the earth;
> to feel the earth beneath each step
>   and behind each gaze at the mountainside;
> to worship on the earth overlooking the earth;
> to draw water and food from the earth
>   and add clothes from the earth;
> to share the earth with its sheep, llamas, cows, dogs,

but especially with its people —
people proud of their earth
but pressed to the earth by people and forces
forgetful of the purposes of the earth;
an Aymara people at one with their earth
and sharing its fruit with me;
to recreate with the earth, climbing its heights
to enjoy its sights more expansively;
to rise with the dawns of the earth
and retire with only its heavenly lights —
thousands in every direction —
protection, promise, presence.
I went to the top of the earth
and found the depths of the earth:
UNITY

Walking in the desert on the outskirts of Tucson, Arizona, after a long winter, both literally and figuratively, I wrote the following reflection entitled "The Psalmist as Shepherd":

How natural to be outdoors, even in the desert wilderness, gravitating toward the sun like the pot-belly cactus, soaking it in, my spirit moving in rhythm with the wind. Then upon the mountain top you spread the clouds and reveal your light. A cloud of witnesses joins in your revelation. I am in your presence. I have come apart to pray, to pause in your presence and give you glory. "Glory to God in the highest and on earth peace" bursts forth. "Have you seen anything?" a passerby asks. "There's a lot to see," I reply, recalling the words I had just read on a trail marker: "The love of the wilderness is more than a hunger for what is always beyond reach; it is also an expression of loyalty to the earth, the only home we shall ever know, the only paradise we ever need — if only we had the eyes to see" (Edward Abbey).

I go to the wilderness seeking you, my God, to be led by your powerful yet gentle love, moved by your Spirit of fire; to pause in your presence; to see your grandeur reflected in the grandeur of your earth; to enter into communion with all of creation. I read on another trail marker: "When we see land as a community to which we belong, we may begin to use it with love and respect" (Aldo Leopold). I understood a little more how Moses must have felt and how the psalmist could sing with such rapture, such emotion. In the wilderness my spirit and voice can literally cry out, can sing your praises aloud.

Get in touch with your own experience of creation and the Creator. List those moments and places where you felt the presence of God and experienced this oneness I have been describing. Go as far back in your life as you want. After completing your list, look it over and see if there are some patterns — particular places or types of places or seasons that have been especially nurturing or revealing. If there are, can you find ways of building them into your life on a regular basis?

"Listen to the Earth with Love in Your Ears"

I find it rewarding to hike in silence and to pause periodically to listen, to be very still and just listen for all the sounds of the earth. I listen in another way to deepen my love for the earth. Friends have begun giving me audio tapes of "earth music." I find this music embeds different senses of the earth deep within my soul. My favorite tape is "Earth Light" by Larkin and Friends. Meditative music can prepare our hearts as well as our heads for encounters with our God, with others, and with creation itself. Music is a powerful instrument for centering.

"Touch the Earth with Love in Your Hands"

"Inch by inch, row by row," sings Pete Seeger, "please bless these seeds I sow. Please keep them safe below as your rain comes tumbling down...." What a splendid way to love the earth gardening provides. "To forget how to dig the earth and tend the soil is to forget ourselves," says Gandhi. What the hands do, the heart will learn. Two friends volunteer a day a week at our local botanical garden to complement their other ministries — education, parenting, hospital chaplaincy. Tilling, planting, weeding, pruning, harvesting, and relishing with our eyes or palates are experiences of caring and communion that carry over to our relationships with animals and people as well.

Hands are for loving touches, not hurtful touches. How many opportunities are there in a day to hold in our hands and appreciate something of creation — a flower, another hand, a pet, a

warm cup of coffee on a cold day, an orange. Learn to peel an
orange slowly. Enjoy its color and shape, a reminder of the sun
and God's warming daily presence in our lives. Enjoy its smell.
As you continue to peel it, realize that just as the orange yields
its true self only when it is peeled, so too we yield our innermost
self only when we are willing to be "peeled." Finally, section
your orange and share the sections with others. Unlike the apple
and many other fruits, an orange begs to be shared. No knife is
required. Our essence, too, and the essence of everything made
in the image of a God who is Generosity-of-Being, is to be broken and shared. I have a poster in my office showing the earth,
with the words: "Love your mother. Work for peace." And I
add: "Handle with Care."

Another way to touch the earth and to "handle our mother
with care" is with stuffed or plastic earth balls. The inflatable
plastic ones are only $5 and are great for tossing around a room or
outside. They don't break things they accidentally hit as readily
as the stuffed, flannel earth balls do. But the stuffed ones, called
"Hugg-a-Planet Earth," are ideal for hugging.[55]* What the hands
do, the heart will learn.

"Walk the Earth with Love in Your Feet"

When I present these thoughts outdoors with children and
adults in warmer weather, we take our shoes and socks off and
feel the earth and the grass with our toes, like some of us did
when we were children. Chief Luther Standing Bear describes
how the old people among the Sioux "came literally to love the
soil and they sat or reclined on the ground with a feeling of being
close to a mothering power. It was good for the skin to touch
the earth and the old people liked to remove their moccasins
and walk with bare feet on the sacred earth. Their tipis were
built on the earth and their altars were made of earth. The birds
that flew in the air came to rest upon the earth and it was the
final abiding place of all things that lived and grew. The soil
was soothing, strengthening, cleansing and healing...."[56] "And
forget not," says Kahlil Gibran in *The Prophet*, "that the earth
delights to feel your bare feet and the winds long to play with
your hair."

We can take care that our feet never intentionally hurt the
earth. I think of those many signs along hiking trails that say

"stay on the trail." No need to trample the fragile vegetation. I notice every time someone has stepped in the carefully laid out gravel patterns in the Japanese Garden. These lines honor the rocks and bushes that they encircle. Footprints destroy the effect.

I can think of no better way to walk the earth with love than to hike in the spirit expressed by Robert Pirsig. It was only recently that I finally learned to hike in this spirit; as my family can attest, I am as compulsive about hiking as I am about everything else. As Pirsig describes it:

> Mountains should be climbed with as little effort as possible and without desire. The reality of your own nature should determine the speed. If you become restless, speed up. If you become winded, slow down. You climb the mountain with an equilibrium between restlessness and exhaustion. Then, when you are no longer thinking ahead, each footstep isn't just a means to an end but a unique event in itself. This leaf has jagged edges. This rock looks loose. From this place the snow is less visible, even though closer. These are things you should notice anyway. To live only for some future goal is shallow. It's the sides of the mountains which sustain life, not the top.... [57]

While walking is excellent exercise, I hope we will also take walks that are not just a means to better physical conditioning. We need Pirsig-type walks that provide experiences of unison among our legs, eyes, lungs, and heart, so that we see and feel what is around us and under our feet.

Other Ways of Living in Harmony with the Earth

What does it mean to live in harmony with the earth on a daily basis, not just in the special moments described above? First, it means building into our regular routine some of these special moments, providing "mini-sabbaticals" for ourselves. Isn't that what God intended in the story of creation, in which the sabbath (from which "sabbatical" comes) is a day to rest and reflect on the goodness of creation? Steve Van Matre invites us: "Come experience the earth with us. Set aside some time each week to get to know your place in space. In addition to being a day of rest, perhaps Sunday should be a day of exploration and discovery for all of us. We need a day dedicated to getting out of our man-made structures, to leaving our urban colonies; a day spent outdoors celebrating the wonders of life; a day cavorting, if you will, in our garden in space."[58]

Just as fasting one day a week can affect us the rest of the week, so too regular outings of celebration and love can bring us into closer harmony with the earth the rest of the week. The possibilities are endless.[59*]

Recycling is an obvious place to start, but not just paper, aluminum, and glass. Family, neighborhood, or church exchanges are helpful for recycling clothing, books, records, toys, or occasionally even tools that can be exchanged or shared. Some groups pool and share services or talents as well. I know of two families that shared a second car. Others have shared major appliances like freezers or tools like lawn-mowers. Such steps help preserve our pocketbooks as well as the earth.

Use less nonrenewable energy sources, heavily packaged goods, nonbiodegradable items. We try to use paper plates and paper towels as seldom as possible and eliminate styrofoam cups and plates altogether. I am starting to get into the habit of taking my coffee mug with me when I go to meetings and workshops and asking organizers of such events to consider alternatives to styrofoam. It's not a big step, but it's a start.

Using public libraries, public parks, and other public facilities helps both pocketbook and the environment. Using such alternatives is an effective way of teaching the environmental ethic and reconciliation with the earth. We learn to take care of books and parks and swings and streams not because we own them, but because others who will come after us will want to use and enjoy them as much as we do. I can hear myself saying this to our small children years ago, as we taped a torn page in a library book before returning it. The earth and all its resources belong to the whole human family and ultimately to God who is the Creator and Sustainer of all species, not just the human species.[60*]

Stewardship

We are stewards of God's creation, not its masters. To "have dominion over all," as we read in the book of Genesis, did not mean exploiting or plundering the earth, using it only for ourselves. As the Presbyterian General Assembly pointed out: "All that justice implies for our own day is equally implied in our responsibility toward those yet to be born. Not only is this earth a gift of God inherited from past generations. We have also 'borrowed it from our children.' We hold it in trust for them. Since we are to pass the earth on to others, we are to be concerned about how we use its resources. We are to resist the tendency to measure success only in terms of growth or to seek fulfillment through the immediate accumulation of things."[61]

If "the earth does not belong to us but we belong to the earth," as Chief Seattle says, then we must approach the earth not with weapons of plunder and domination but unarmed and full of peace. This is another of Francis's insights that Carlo Carretto has put into words: "Here is the miracle of love: to discover that all creation is one, flung out into space by a God who is a Father [Mother], and that if you present yourself to it as God does — unarmed and full of peace — creation will recognize you and meet you with a smile."[62] If we approach the earth with a smile on our face, a song in our hearts or on our lips, and hands open in a stance of vulnerability and peace, we will love and be loved more deeply by this "mother" with whom we are one.

Our stance toward creation is not just one of caring in the sense of not harming, nor is it only the unarmed and peaceful stance of the child before its mother. It is also the active one of being on the leading edge, as it were, of the universe's unfolding of itself. I read Brian Swimme's *The Universe Is a Green Dragon* for a second time during a visit to the Manzanos of New Mexico. In that setting, the universe came alive for me in a whole new way and my role in its ongoing creation crystallized as never before.[63]*

Brian sees God as "Ultimate Generosity" and speaks of the "Supreme Being's ontological desire to pour forth goodness, to share and ignite being spontaneously..." (pp. 145–146). The universe, as the fruit of this creative pouring out of itself that is God, can itself be best described as "generosity-of-being." We are then "generosity-of-being evolved into human form." We are the leading edge of creativity in this moment of the universe's creation. In Brian's poetic and empowering language, "We are the space where the earth dreams" (p. 138). "Whatever you deeply feel demands to be given form and released. Profound joy insists upon song and dance.... Learn to sing, learn to see your life and work as a song by the universe. Dance! See your most ordinary activities as the dance of the galaxies and all living beings..." (pp. 147–148). "Plunge into the work of living as 'surprise become aware of itself'" (p. 123).

So, "fling your gifts into the world..." (p. 148). "We ignite life in others" and "we become beauty to ignite the beauty of others..." (pp. 61, 79). "Lure others into similar moments of seeing.... Yes, we awake to fascination and we strive to fascinate. We work to enchant others. We work to ignite life, to evoke presence, to enhance the unfolding of being. All of this is the actuality of love" (pp. 56–57). The cosmos itself is on a journey:

As we lie in bed each morning, we awake to the fire that created all the stars. Our principal moral act is to cherish this fire, the source of our transformation, our selves, our society, our species, and our planet. In each moment, we face this cosmic responsibility: are we tending this fire; revering it? Are we creating something beautiful for our planetary home? This is the central fire of your self, the central fire of the entire cosmos; it must not be wasted on trivialities or revenge, resentment or despair. We have the power to forge cosmic fire. What can compare with such a destiny? (pp. 169–170)

Pray with me for some of that vision and cosmic fire, that we might see the significance of every tiny creative act we do each day, that we might each be a more compassionate and courageous instrument of God's fiery love: *"Come, Holy Spirit, fill the hearts of your faithful and enkindle in us the fire of your love. Send forth your Spirit, Lord, and we will be re-created and you will transform — through us — the face of the earth."*

For Reflection

I conclude simply with Francis's majestic hymn of praise, "Canticle of All Creation":

Most High, all powerful, all Good Lord! All praise is yours, all glory, all honor, and all blessing. To you alone, Most high, do they belong. No mortal lips are worthy to pronounce your name.

All praise be yours, my Lord, through all that you have made, and first my Lord Brother Sun, who brings the day, and light you give us through him. How beautiful is he, how radiant in all his splendor! Of you, Most High, he bears the likeness.

All praise be yours, my Lord, through Sister Moon and Stars, in the heavens you have made them bright and precious and fair.

All praise be yours, my Lord, through Brother Wind and Air, fair and stormy, all the weather's moods, by which you cherish all that you have made.

All praise be yours, my Lord, through Sister Water, so useful, lowly, precious and pure.

All praise be yours, my Lord, through Brother Fire, through whom you brighten up the night. How beautiful he is, how gay. Full of power and strength.

All praise be yours, my Lord, through Sister Earth, our Mother, who feeds us in her sovereignty and produces various fruits with colored flowers and herbs.

All praise be yours, my Lord, through those who grant pardon for love of you; those who endure sickness and trial, happy those who endure in peace, by you, the Most High, they will be crowned.

All praise be yours, my Lord, through Sister Death, from whose embrace no mortal can escape. Woe to those who die in sin. Happy those she finds doing your will. The second death can do no harm to them.

Praise and bless the Lord, and give thanks. And serve with great humility.[64]

Chapter 9

"Love Your Mother, Work for Peace"

The peace movement and the environmental movement have come together in the realization that the entire planet is in danger from the arms race. The U.S. Catholic bishops put it starkly: "In the nuclear arsenals of the United States or the Soviet Union alone, there exists a capacity to do something no other age could imagine: we can threaten the entire planet" (*The Challenge of Peace*, no. 122). No wonder the U.S. Methodist bishops entitled their prophetic document *In Defense of Creation*. The human community, indeed the whole of creation, faces "a new moment." We are privileged and burdened to be aware of this "moment of supreme crisis."

A former military chaplain at the Alamogordo desert base in New Mexico where the atomic bomb was tested gave me a packet of crystals he had picked up from the area where the bombs were exploded. It was God's earth — desert sand — transformed into greenish crystals. Here were products and symbols of the desecration of the earth, the rape of our mother. I arranged these crystals in a tiny case and placed them on the shelf in the prayer corner of our living room.

What can we do to defend our mother earth, to reverse the arms race, and to prevent these weapons of such terrible destruction from ever being used? Promoting North American–Soviet friendship is one important place to start.

Six Steps for Making Enemies into Friends

A special issue of *Sojourners* magazine ("Where East Meets West," February 1987) was entirely devoted to this very question of U.S.-U.S.S.R. relations. In "Breaking the Power" Danny Collum wrote on the need to confront the powers and principalities that keep our nations locked in an escalating race toward "mutually assured destruction," or "MAD," as our policy of nuclear deterrence is described; he reinforced my sense that I had to do something. But it was Jim Forest's article "Our Mutual Humanity — Fostering Friendship with the 'Enemy'" that really started me on my journey with the people of the Soviet Union.

Jim suggested starting with reading. He recommended several novels, histories, and travel books. Given my mental state at the time, I felt I could handle only a travel book. It led to a Yevgeny Yevtushenko novel (since I had admired a poem he wrote). I didn't like the novel, but I felt I should not turn back. I picked up Harrison Salisbury's graphic account of the siege of Leningrad by the Germans between 1941 and 1944, entitled *900 Days*. This had a profound impact on me. I had heard often that some 20 million Soviet people died in the "Great Patriotic War," as the Soviet people call World War II, and that that experience had so seared itself into their consciousness that they desperately want to avoid war with us or any other country. But I did not have a real feel for that consciousness — I had not gotten into the "soul" of the Soviet people — until I read Salisbury's book. That book was pivotal in my journey.

Step 1: Seeing Their Faces

Soon I discovered a number of "reconciliation projects" offered by the U.S.-U.S.S.R. Reconciliation Program of the Fellowship of Reconciliation. Among these are a slide show, a set of posters, and a set of postcards all entitled "Forbidden Faces." In one of those Daniel Berrigan writes, "There are very few of us in America who are able to see the faces of Soviet children, of Soviet workers, or old people, or students. Let us see the faces of one another, especially the faces which are forbidden us, forbidden our eyes and forbidden our hearts." I was one of the vast majority who had not seen the faces of Soviet people, much less met any. Gross stereotypes I had seen — the movie *Rocky IV*, commercials for Pepsi and Wendy's that made fun of Soviets, the TV special "Amerika." "It's okay, Dad; they only kill the enemy," my son David, then nine years old, had told me after seeing an Army recruiting film in the fourth grade. Maybe I could use these posters and cards to counteract such stereotypes and begin to put faces on our "enemy." As soon as we begin to see our enemy as a grandmother, a worker, a parent, a child, and not an impersonal object or worse (for instance as an "evil empire"), then we might start to question a policy that threatens to "nuke 'em."

I hung a poster depicting Soviet people in my office and began to encourage teachers and pastors to do so in their classrooms and the vestibules of their churches. I sent postcards to my Congressional representatives and friends and urged them to work toward building bridges between our two nations, instead of fueling the arms race even more. When I was questioned about why a picture of Soviet people was appropriate in a church building, I responded with Paul's words in 2 Corinthians: As "ambassadors of Christ," we are "ambassadors of reconciliation" wherever the body of Christ is broken, fractured. Nowhere is this truer than between the U.S. and the U.S.S.R.

A beautiful postcard from the Fellowship of Reconciliation was the next step. On it is printed a prayer for peace in English and Russian. The text in English reads:

> Lead me from death to life, from falsehood to truth.
> Lead me from despair to hope, from fear to trust.
> Lead me from hate to love, from war to peace.
> Let peace fill our heart, our world, our universe....

It became our Christmas card — a low-profile way of sharing our peace concern with people who might not agree with our politics but who would agree with us that we all need to pray for peace. I learned a couple of Russian words because of the postcard, which began another leg in the journey.

Before going on to further external steps, I want to share the internal realization I was coming to at this point in my journey. I had always been taught that because we are "one body" in Christ, what one part did affected the whole. I began to see myself as a potential embodiment of the unity of two peoples deeply divided. If I could "take in" the reality and "soul" of the Soviet people in some way, I could begin to embody in my own person the unity I wanted to effect in the world.

Step 2: Learning the Language

Kathy and I travelled to the Soviet Union with a "Peacemaking Program" delegation from the Presbyterian Church USA, as part of a larger National Council Churches delegation to cele-

brate the millennium of Christianity in what is now the the Soviet Union. In preparation for this July 1988 trip, but also as part
of my earlier decision to pursue more of a "Russian consciousness," I began to learn the Russian language, along with more
literature, music, history.

Even if I could speak only a little of the language, I felt I
would be drawn into the lives and reality of the Soviet people
much more than if I didn't know any Russian. Fellow "pilgrims"
who hadn't learned any Russian soon regretted it.

Step 3: Singing Together

If a few of the Russian words you learn are in a song, you
can take step three: singing together. It's hard to stay enemies or
strangers if you sing together. The most popular peace song in the
Soviet Union was written by a five-year-old boy from Moscow.
The Russian and English words and notes are simple. You may
have heard Pete Seeger sing it. Many children in the U.S. are
learning the song as part of bridge-building programs such as
the "Peace Child" play and movement.[65]

MAY THERE ALWAYS BE SUNSHINE

English:	May there always be sunshine
	May there always be blue skies
	May there always be mama (papa)
	May there always be me (we).
Russian:	Poost tsegda boodyit solnse
	Poost tsegda boodyit nieba
	Poost tsegda boodyit mama (y papa)
	Poost tsegda boodoo ya (mwe).

Step 4: Gift-giving

The fourth step in becoming friends is to exchange gifts. Peace
buttons, decals, friendship bookmarks, origami peace cranes,
postcards, family pictures, and prayer cards are easy to carry or
mail, inexpensive, greatly appreciated, and readily available from
the Fellowship of Reconciliation and others.

Each of these steps, except singing together, you can take
whether or not you have the chance to visit the Soviet Union.
Pen-pals are one way to do this, although mail is not very reliable

in the U.S.S.R. and correspondence relationships are sometimes frustrating.[66*]

More and more groups of Soviet citizens are travelling to North America, as the reverse is also happening. Probably your community has had Soviet visitors. Hosting a Soviet visitor for a meal is fun, no matter what your language ability is. Many U.S. communities have a Soviet-American Friendship Society group that would know of pending visits.[67]

Step 5: Dancing

The fifth step in making friends requires physical presence, but it can be done wherever different peoples are gathered together. Taking Brian Swimme's injunction to heart, we can dance. Any "melody of God" worth its salt (and that has not lost its flavor) should be willing, in fact eager, to dance. I have to confess that I am a very reluctant dancer, so if I can do it, you can do it. Try this traditional Russian folk song and dance, celebrating the wonder of creation. In translation, the song goes like this, with dancers in a circle holding hands: "If all people lived their lives [dancers take four steps to the right] as if they were a song [four steps to the left], they'd provide music for the stars [two steps in, held hands up; two steps back lowering hands] to dance circles in the night" [drop hands; turn individual circles; end with a double clap]. The message? If all of us would live our lives with vitality, we would provide such powerful "music" that the stars would be affected. Instead of just twinkling, they'd start dancing in circles. If we radiated such life and joy, we would affect the whole cosmos.

Step 6: Prayer

A final step is prayer with and for one another. You can use the Fellowship of Reconciliation prayer above. Or use the litany that the Russian Orthodox church uses every Sunday in praying for us, for the President of the United States, and for peace between our countries and for the whole earth. As many as 65 million Russian Orthodox Christians pray this litany [to each petition for peace, add the response: Lord, have mercy]:

- In peace, let us pray to the Lord.
- For the peace from above, and for our salvation, let us pray to the Lord.

- For the peace of the whole world; for the welfare of the holy churches of God, and for the unity of all people, let us pray to the Lord.

- For this holy community of faith, and for those who with faith, reverence, and love of God enter herein, let us pray to the Lord.

- For our pastor(s), for all clergy, for all who bear office in the church, for all of the people of God in all times and places, let us pray to the Lord.

- For the President of the United States of America and all civil authorities, for the leaders of all nations and for those who serve in the United Nations, let us pray to the Lord.

- That God will aid them and grant them wisdom and strength to struggle for justice and peace.

- For this community, and for every city and land, and for the faithful who dwell in them, let us pray to the Lord.

- For healthful seasons, for abundance of the fruits of the earth and for peaceful times, let us pray to the Lord.

- For travelers by sea, by land and by air; for the sick and the suffering; for refugees and the homeless; for prisoners and their salvation; for the poor and the needy, let us pray to the Lord.

- For our deliverance from all tribulation, wrath, danger and necessity, let us pray to the Lord.

- Help us; save us; have mercy upon us and keep us, O God, by your grace.

- Calling to remembrance our mothers and fathers in the faith, with all of God's saints, let us commend ourselves and each other, and all our life unto Christ our God.

- To you, O Lord.

- O Lord, our God, whose power is beyond anything that we can imagine, whose glory is greater than our ability to know, whose mercy knows no limits, and whose love toward humankind is deeper than our capacity to understand: Do, O God, in your tender compassion look upon this holy community of faith and grant us and those who pray with us your rich blessings and benefits. For unto you are due all glory, honor and worship: to the Father, and to the Son, and to the Holy Spirit: now and ever and unto ages of ages. Amen.

Richard Deats, longtime director of the Fellowship of Reconciliation's U.S.-U.S.S.R. Reconciliation Program, has offered a third prayer:

> O Divine Spirit,
> whose Light fills the Universe and all living things,
> we lift up to your presence

Mikhail Gorbachev and George Bush.
Illumine them. Inspire their decisions.
Guide their actions —
that the nations they lead
may turn from the insanity of the arms race
to the healing of the earth
and the meeting of human needs. Amen.

Peace Cranes

The paper peace crane has become a very special peace symbol for me. In the context of our reconciliation with the earth, its symbolism is striking. Sadako Sasaki, the eleven-year-old Japanese girl from Hiroshima who made cranes famous, was a victim of the same atomic bomb that transformed her city into rubble in an instant and transformed God's desert sand into the green crystals I have in my prayer corner. Sadako tried to make a thousand of these cranes after her school mate had told her the Japanese legend that making a thousand cranes would bring her long life.

Sadako was dying from leukemia from the radiation from the bomb dropped on her city when she was only two. She completed 644 before she died in 1955. On the last crane that she made, she wrote "PEACE" on its wings and told it to fly over the whole world. Her classmates completed the first thousand cranes. The city of Hiroshima erected a monument to Sadako in the Peace Park. People all over the world, especially children, have been making Sadako's peace cranes ever since. Strands of a thousand cranes hang from Sadako's thirty-foot arch memorial in the Peace Park. Peace cranes are sent to government leaders worldwide as symbols and petitions for peace policies. They are given as friendship gifts, as presents to loved ones on special days connected with peace.

I took peace cranes to the Soviet Union as friendship gifts and discovered how special they were. They are known all over the Soviet Union as a *"golub mira"* ("peace bird"). They became my gift in my six-step process for turning enemies into friends. They are also wonderful enclosures in letters to Soviet friends.

The Piskariovskoye Memorial Cemetery in Leningrad was the place in the U.S.S.R. that I wanted to visit more than any other

and the place where the peace cranes took on a special significance. Here are buried more than 500,000 victims of the 900-day
siege. One million Leningraders (of a total population of 2.5 million) died in those 900 days, most of starvation. I had just read
Soviet poet Vera Inber's moving *Leningrad Diary* and could thus
feel something of what that tragedy meant. Alla was the In-
tourist guide on our delegation's visit to the cemetery to lay our
wreathes of sorrow and peace. I found myself standing next to
Alla after our service, still facing the statue of "Mother Russia"
at the foot of the memorial.

Knowing she was a Leningrader, I asked whether she personally experienced the siege. She said she was a baby at the beginning of the siege and with thousands of other children was evac-
uated from the city. Her father died somewhere "at the front,"
as she put it, a month later (October 1941). "And his body was
never recovered," she added. Her mother was left alone to endure the 900 days. "It must have been very difficult for her, as I
think about it now," she concluded succinctly. We stood together
in silence. I put my arm around her. We were one in a special
moment of communion.

Eventually I told her that many North Americans truly care
and are working that this tragedy never be repeated. At that,
she looked me in the eye and said softly, "Yes, you care. In
every group I bring here there are one or two who truly care." I
wanted to protest that her estimates were probably much too low,
but instead I absorbed her somber assessment and implied plea
that I do more to increase that number of truly caring people.
I had agreed to teach other members of our delegation how to
make the paper cranes right after the memorial service, and so I
left Alla. I walked back and there, right across from the eternal
flame memorializing the victims of the siege, I taught six others
how to fold the paper cranes.

As I told Sadako's story, I kept thinking of Alla. Each fold of
that crane planted another seed of solidarity in my heart. What
my hands were doing, my heart was learning. I continue to
make and teach others to make these cranes, but now with more
understanding of what the *golub mira* stands for. Each crane is a
recommitment to answer Sadako's plea that no other child have
to suffer her kind of death, a recommitment to be an answer to
Alla's plea.[68]

For Reflection

1. Is this a good time in your life to take a step toward becoming an embodiment of solidarity between the peoples of your country and the Soviet Union? Which step makes the most sense and will lead to other steps? I am not presuming that you should make this a priority in your reconciliation efforts. There are many other huge divisions in the human community that need healing, including those in our own families. We have to remember our limits.

2. Jesus' words on loving our enemies (Matt. 5:43–48; Luke 6:27–35) and the parable of the good Samaritan (Luke 10:29–37) remind us of how wide the reach of our compassion must extend. Both the Catholic and Methodist bishops' documents have prophetic sections devoted to the need and possibility for a new relationship between the U.S. and the U.S.S.R. and to a biblical vision of peace that embraces the whole human community and the earth itself.

3. Pray with me that all may be one, that we may be one as Jesus and God are one (John 17:21). I composed the following prayer one morning at sunrise on the Black Sea. I was standing in front the eternal flame memorializing the war dead from the Soviet city of Odessa, where the rising sun reminded me of God's flaming presence in our lives and of our sacred mission of becoming ambassadors of reconciliation:

ETERNAL FLAMES AT DAWN

Once more Your Spirit is poured out over your world,
a Spirit of reconciliation between our peoples,
with the earth itself.
This eternal flame in the city of Odessa
inspires us to renounce violence and build bridges
as the way of remembering — re-membering,
making us one again, members of one body, your body, Jesus.

An eternal flame at sunrise —
your daily reminder of your loving presence
warming, guiding us.
Lead us in your light, O Lord,
to renounce war, hatred, mistrust
and to step across those barriers of language and ideology

and to meet as family.
Re-member us, O Lord,
as you remind us of the powerful presence
of your Spirit, the fire of your love.
"Come, Holy Spirit, fill the hearts of your faithful
and enkindle in us the fire of your love.
Send forth your Spirit, Lord,
and we will be re-created, re-membered,
and you, through us, will renew, transform, the face of the earth."

Chapter 10

Solidarity as Resistance

The prophet is both social critic and energizer, denouncing injustice and violence and offering a vision of hope. Both are essential, but it is denunciation that "resistance" points to first. I heard the call to embrace this prophetic ministry in a moment of special clarity during a public vigil against United States policy in Central America. The vigil included a reading from the Hebrew prophet Ezekiel:

> The word of Adonai was addressed to me as follows, "Son of man, speak to the members of your nation. Say to them, 'When I send the sword against a country, the people of that country select one of themselves and post him as a sentry; if the sentry sees the sword coming against the country, he sounds the horn to alert the people. If someone hears the sound of the horn, but pays no attention, the sword will overtake him and destroy him; he will have been responsible for his own death. He has heard the sound of the horn, and paid no attention....
> " 'If, however, the sentry has seen the sword coming but has not blown the horn, and so the people are not alerted and the sword overtakes them and destroys one of them, the latter shall indeed die for his sin, but I will hold the sentry responsible for his death.' Son of man, I have appointed you as sentry for My people" (Ezek. 33:1–7).

Sentries for God's People

I heard myself and all other people of faith addressed in that passage. We are all called to be sentries. And I see the sword coming, and not just in the possibility of nuclear destruction or environmental collapse. It has already come in the form of starvation for millions every year. The Vatican was eminently clear in its 1976 response to the United Nations' call for disarmament: "The arms race is an act of aggression that amounts to a crime; for even if these weapons are not used, by their cost alone, they kill the poor by causing them to starve."

Wasteful military spending means that one child dies every two seconds. Add to that what physicist Rosalie Bertell estimates are the more than 17 million casualties worldwide from the testing of nuclear weapons. And think of the millions of young people who despair about the future because they believe nuclear war is likely to destroy their world.[69*] The sword has come indeed.

I have to "sound the horn and alert the people." What about you? Do you have that sense of urgency? Do you see other manifestations of the "sword" that you think the people need to hear about? Because this clearly takes us into the public arena, you might feel a little anxious at this point. I do.

To help us deal with our anxiety, though, let's remember that we are not "lone sentries," in three senses. First, God is with us. The first chapter of Jeremiah proclaims this loudly. Second, there is "a cloud of witnesses" hovering over us.[70*] The presence of Gandhi, Francis, Dorothy Day, Martin Luther King, Archbishop Romero, Jean Donovan, and others in the "company of saints" does hover over us. We need only allow ourselves to become aware of that empowering reality.

And there is a third sense in which we are not alone. Very few "resisters" I know are in it by themselves. Usually they are part of what are called "affinity groups." Dom Helder Camara, prophetic Brazilian Catholic bishop, has called such groups "Abrahamic minorities." He urges us to keep attuned to our pilgrim status and stop worrying about our small numbers. Sometimes these groups are intentional communities like Jim and Shelley Douglass's Ground Zero "collective." Others are less intense support groups that come together at least monthly, often around specific actions or campaigns. Generally the most helpful ones are those that combine prayer, lifestyle reflection, study, action, and celebration — focusing more holistically rather than just on a specific action. To move further into resistance and be more faithful "sentries" for God's people, we need to have this kind of support system.

Connections

Resistance and Affirmation: A Yes to Balance the No

There is a connection between resistance to evil — saying no — and building alternative ways of living — saying yes. An integral person embodies both. The prophetic denunciation of injustice needs to be coupled with prophetic affirmations of life and announcements of hope.

The beauty of the lives of Francis and Dorothy Day, Martin Luther King and Jean Donovan, for instance, is that their joyful service with the poor was such an affirmation of life. Compassionate and courageous Nicaraguans, Salvadorans, and Guatemalans rebuild their villages and lives as they resist the destructiveness of violence and oppression. Some U.S. inner-city groups create their own credit unions, food coops, and clinics at the same time they challenge city hall, banks, and corporations to provide essential services. As Henri Nouwen so perceptively puts it, "Only a loving heart, a heart that continues to affirm life at all times and places, can say 'no' to death without being corrupted by it. A heart that loves friends and enemies is a heart that calls forth life and lifts up life to be celebrated. It is a heart that refuses to dwell in death because it is always enchanted with the abundance of life. Indeed only in the context of this strong loving yes to life can the power of death be overcome."[71]

The Giant Triplets of Militarism, Racism, and Materialism

While "peace" and "justice" are clearly linked in the biblical vision of Shalom, groups focused primarily on one of the couplet have not always seen the need to work on the other or even work in coalition with groups committed to the other. Dr. King came to see the essential connections between racism, militarism, and materialism in the 1960s. He was widely criticized within the civil rights movement for his public denunciations of the Vietnam War. "This will cost us many allies," he was told repeatedly. Yet his prophetic voice continued to cry out against the dragons of both racism and militarism, with which he combined the dragon of materialism, for he had sensed their close connections: "I am convinced that if we are to get on the right side of the world revolution, we as a nation must undergo a radical revolution of values. We must rapidly begin the shift from a 'thing-oriented' society to a 'person-oriented' society. When machines and computers, profit motives and property rights are considered more important than people, the giant triplets of racism, materialism and militarism are incapable of being conquered."[72]

It is important to be clear about what we are up against. In his letter to the Ephesians Paul describes the battle and the nonviolent character of the weapons we are to take up:

Finally, grow strong in the Lord, with the strength of his power. Put God's armour on so as to be able to resist the devil's tactics. For it is not against human enemies that we have to struggle, but against the Powers and Principalities who originate the darkness in this world, the spiritual army of evil in the heavens. That is why you must rely on God's armour, or you will not be able to put up any resistance when the worst happens, or have enough resources to hold your ground. So stand your ground, with truth buckled round your waist, and integrity for a breastplate, wearing for shoes on your feet the eagerness to spread the gospel of peace and always carrying the shield of faith so that you can use it to put out the burning arrows of the evil one. And then you must accept salvation from God to be your helmet and receive the word of God from the Spirit to use as a sword. (Eph. 6:10–17)

In our own time, these Powers and Principalities could rightly be identified as demonic forces that have so invaded and embedded themselves in our ways of thinking and our institutions that it will take much more than rational argumentation to root them out. These Powers and Principalities are the dragons of our day. Some have become "idols" as well.[73]* Before we look at ways we can resist these Powers and Principalities, it is important to realize how far into resistance we have already gone.

Resisting the "Powers and Principalities"

How many times have you already resisted the societal imperative to consume more, to give in to convenience and use all those "disposables"? How many other "selfish" desires have you resisted — with regard to eating and drinking, to retaliating against those who have wronged you, to other "cravings"? Have you resisted government leaders' efforts to have you think of the people of the Soviet Union as our "enemies" and their country as an "evil empire"?

Have you resisted racist, sexist, and hateful comments and jokes, by choosing not to believe them? You've probably had the courage at times to challenge such comments in conversations with friends, associates, or family. You may have resisted the impulse to fight back hurtfully and even challenged others who were fighting that way to try a different approach. I wouldn't be surprised if your political leaders, maybe even your religious leaders, have heard from you because you refuse to remain silent in the face of the dragons. We are not starting from scratch. But let's allow ourselves to be pushed a little further.

Shelley and Jim Douglass are good people to lead us further into resistance. They live alongside the train tracks, next to the U.S. Naval Submarine Base at Bangor, Washington, tracks on which travel the nuclear materials used on Trident submarines. They have chosen to confront the dragon of militarism directly and for a lifetime. In her essay, "The Power of Noncooperation," Shelley writes:

> As citizens of the United States, we are complicit in the wrongs done by our country. It is important to identify the points at which we directly support these wrongs, and withdraw our support. It is also important to end our silence about them. Other people need to know what is happening, and need to know that people are opposing it. Demonstrations and civil disobedience are a part of this breaking of the silence, as are letter-writing and lobbying campaigns. Speaking and acting against what is wrong creates a community of people who can come together to support each other and to perpetuate what is best in their traditions.
>
> Sometimes noncooperation is more subtle than marches, less direct than tax refusal. Sometimes noncooperation may simply mean refusing to allow our minds to be manipulated, our hearts to be controlled. Refusing to hate the Russians is noncooperation. Continuing to differentiate between a repressive government, which we may oppose, and its people, who are our sisters and brothers — is noncooperation. Remembering the strengths of our tradition is also noncooperation — insistence on democracy, ideals of free education, of food and

clothing for everyone, of work with dignity, of respect for all races....

The discipline of nonviolence requires of us that we move into these various forms of noncooperation. We will probably move slowly, one step at a time. Each step will lead to another step. Each step will be a withdrawal from support of what is wrong and at the same time a building of an alternative. Negativity is never enough. It is not enough to oppose the wrong without suggesting the right. Our religious roots can help us here, with their insistence on confronting the evil within ourselves and on our unity with all peoples.[74]

Let's look at how we can apply this noncooperation with evil to the dragons of materialism, technologism, militarism, nationalism, and racism.

Materialism and Technologism

Many people in the affluent First World have made materialism their idol, whether it is named "consumption" or "maximization of profit."[75] In their prophetic 1975 pastoral letter *This Land Is Home to Me*, the Catholic bishops of Appalachia write:

The way of life which these corporate giants create is called by some "technological rationalization." Its forces contain promise.... Too often, however, its forces become perverted, hostile to the dignity of the earth and of its people. Its destructive growth patterns pollute the air, foul the water, rape the land. The driving force behind this perversion is "Maximization of Profit," a principle which too often converts itself into an idolatrous power. This power overwhelms the good intentions of noble people.... Of course technological rationalization and the profit principle have served important functions in human development. It is not they themselves that form an idol, but the idol is formed when they become absolutes and fail to yield, when the time has come, to other principles.... Profit over people is an idol. And it is not a new idol, for Jesus long ago warned us, "No one can be the slave of two masters ... You cannot be the slave both of God and money" (Matthew 6:24).[76]

What I called "technologism" and the Appalachian bishops "technological rationalization" is the notion that technology is god, that it can solve all our problems. I have heard it called the "technological imperative" — "if something can be done, it ought to be done," no other values to be considered in the decision. The bishops rightly speak of the "promise" of technology, that it is not an idol in itself, but that it can become an idol.

We looked at ways to resist consumerism and technologism in chapters 6 and 8. We can also resist advertising. We can point out the manipulation of advertising to others as we drive past billboards or watch TV together.[77]

Militarism

Archbishop Hunthausen of Seattle has prophetically resisted the idol of militarism, and he has paid a price. He writes:

> We have to refuse to give incense — in our day, tax dollars — to our nuclear idol. . . . Form 1040 is the place where the Pentagon enters all of our lives, and asks our unthinking cooperation with the idol of nuclear destruction. I think the teaching of Jesus tells us to render to a nuclear-armed Caesar what that Caesar deserves — tax resistance. And to begin to render to God alone that complete trust which we now give, through our tax dollars, to a demonic form of power. Some would call what I am urging "civil disobedience." I prefer to see it as obedience to God.

The Hebrew prophets repeatedly condemned reliance on military fortifications and alliances instead of trusting in God (see Hos. 7 and 8, 10:13–14, 12:7; Jer. 2:37; Isa. 7:9, 22:8–14, 26:7–19, 30:1–18, 31:1–3). Tax resistance is a difficult issue for most people. Kathy and I have wrestled with it for years.[78*] Religious peacemaking groups provide action suggestions in this area as well as group support.[79*] Many of the nonviolent resistance campaigns involve civil disobedience. Like tax resistance, other forms of civil disobedience are probably just as troubling to you.[80*]

Earlier I mentioned "physical accompaniment," describing how "internationals" accompany those in danger from their own governments or para-military forces. Ron Sider is trying to enlist "a few good men and women" for a "peace brigade."[81] These are people willing to go to places of conflict and place themselves in the midst of the conflict as examples of nonviolence, much as Gandhi did in the midst of the Hindu-Moslem conflagrations. Some of Gandhi's followers continued this tradition of peace brigades, calling them *shanti senas*. Witness for Peace in Nicaragua, now spreading to other Central American countries, has a similar vision and purpose. People of nonviolence can resist violence, especially that violence sponsored by their own government, by placing themselves between the executioners of that violence and their victims. Brian Willson and others have been doing that at the Concord Naval Air Station in Northern California, blocking the trains carrying the weapons of this violence toward Central America. For that resistance, Brian was almost killed when a train severed his legs. He gave his legs that victims of U.S.-sponsored terrorism in Central America might be spared further loss of their limbs and life. Brian's example is heroic, I know, but I think it is what we are ultimately called to, maybe not in the same way, but at least with the same willingness to sacrifice ourselves for others.

There are links between our interior struggles and our societal resistance. Retaliation is a desire we all experience. I have to resist this desire within myself if I am to have any credibility in confronting it in U.S. policy. How do I challenge the behavior of my children without putting them down personally, without trying to "get even" with them, without threatening to unload my arsenal of punishments if they don't shape up? My efforts as a male to nurture gentleness in myself and other males, to develop the nurturing side of our persons, are part of this process.

Why it is so hard to think of alternatives to retaliation and domination? Part of the problem lies within us, with our sinful condition. But part of it lies in the values, mindset, policies, and institutions of our society that have been so penetrated by the Powers and Principalities that we are locked in a spiritual struggle far beyond human instruments. The U.S. mindset says that invulnerability is a "must." Vulnerability and trust in God are absurd to most policy makers. Unthinkable that any "window of vulnerability" not be immediately shut tight, even if shutting it means escalating an arms race that actually makes us more vulnerable and insecure, rather than less. The invasion of Grenada, the bombing of Libya, mining harbors in Nicaragua are all celebrated as the righteous wielding of national power rather than being condemned as unjust attacks to be confessed. Despite the urgings of our churches, we still have not found the national will to repent over the bombings of Hiroshima and Nagasaki.

The U.S. is infected with policies like Manifest Destiny and the Monroe Doctrine; it tolerates the frontier ethic where vigilante justice was widespread; it tolerates the violation of women as much as the violation of the environment. To live and preach forgiveness, gentleness, vulnerability, and nonviolence is not the "American way." But precisely because it is so difficult, it is even more imperative that we commit ourselves to doing our best.

Nationalism and Racism

I have put these two ism's together because the dynamics are similar in both and both are closely connected with militarism. Expressions like "white supremacy," "master race," and "apartheid" reflect the same desire to be on top, in control, "number one" that is at the heart of nationalism become an end in itself. Nationalism can be a positive force, a stepping stone between tribal or community loyalties and a sense of the international community or human family. But nationalism can also become an idol in which survival of one's nation-state can justify the destruction of the rest of the world. Domination, power over others, has often become an idol in human history, and is one we have to contend with in our time as well.

I was deeply moved when I visited Dachau on Memorial Day, 1986, for I saw there the horrifying results not only of racism but of nationalism as well. The plaque at the entrance of the central building reads in four languages, "Never Again," which became my commitment. To me, Dachau means "never again" should any members of the human family inflict such suffering on our fellow human beings. Franz Jaegerstatter, the Austrian who refused to serve in Hitler's army, was executed. His widow (living not far from Dachau) still suffers recrimination today from those who see resistance as treason. When the nation becomes "god," those entranced by the idol view treason as the ultimate sin. Memorial Day should not be an idolatrous celebration of nationalism, but a recommitment to resist human suffering and evil in the name of its victims and inspired by the memory of those who resisted with their lives.

At Dachau 200,000 Jews died, over 30,000 of whom were executed, and countless Russian prisoners died there too, as did more than 2500 Catholic priests who protested their church's silence. We resist Dachau in Central America when we challenge U.S.-sponsored violence and provide sanctuary for its victims, when we "witness for peace" side-by-side with those resisting. We resist Dachau, the incineration of those dehumanized as godless enemies, when we challenge nuclear holocaust and reach out as sister and brother to the peoples of the Soviet Union and promote the breaking down of barriers as well as bombs. We resist Dachau and remember its victims when we promote policies that balance the rights of both Jews and Palestinians to security and space to live, ultimately as one. We resist Dachau each time we dare to cross the barriers of language, nationality, race, ideology, and religion in order to embrace one another.

Resisting racism in our own country has become a true imperative for me and many others. There are many ways we can construct the positive alternative of a multiracial lifestyle and society. I recently attended the funeral of the fiancée of one of our staff members. The death was violent and unexpected and the pain devastating to those close to the victim. But the witness of faith and compassion in the Black Baptist church was a gift I did not anticipate. How often do those of us who are white take the opportunity to worship with an African-American congregation and experience their faith and compassion? I haven't very often, but the few times I have done so have been special experiences of God's Shalom. No matter what our race or religion, we can worship more inclusively. This requires finding persons who can help us, seeking out places and times appropriate for such experiences. The following "personal affirmative action program" is primarily for white adults, but it is applicable to every racial group and can be adapted to families or groups.

- In what ways could you make your home, room, office, rectory/parsonage more multicultural in terms of the pictures on the walls, the reading materials on the tables, the guests you invite in? And what about the music you listen to?

- Are there acquaintances or work associates from different racial groups you could cultivate as friends? We make decisions about friendships all the time. Why not add racial diversity to the criteria we currently operate with?

- What opportunities are available to you to use members of other racial groups for professional services — doctors, dentists, lawyers, educators, coaches, ministers, case workers? This can help break down the stereotype of "minority inferiority" and overcome fears.

- Are there minority suppliers in your community for your regular purchases, from hardware and school and office supplies to baked goods and meat? Many U.S. urban communities have directories of minority suppliers, sometimes called the "Black Pages." You might consider a bank's hiring practices and its lending policies — for example, does it refuse to make loans to the poor or people of color — among the criteria you use in selecting your bank. Challenging those who discriminate and rewarding those who do not (by giving them your business) are important resistance actions.

- Encouraging stores to provide multiracial greeting cards, toys, and books is not unrealistic because these goods are available. Often persons responsible for purchasing do not hear from consumers that they want such products. Are such items available where you shop? Have you checked? In toy stores, you might start with dolls. In stationery and drug stores, you might start with greeting cards.

- What resources are there to help you appreciate the positive contributions of people of color? Educational experiences could include good TV shows (for example, "The Cosby Show"), videos, and TV specials. Occasionally these specials focus on minority heroes whose special days we can also celebrate. Martin Luther King's birthday is the most obvious example. What could you do to celebrate his birthday in a way that could deepen your multiracial sensitivity and link you with King's commitment to confront militarism, materialism, and racism?

- Cultural events offer rich possibilities for nurturing solidarity. What opportunities are there in your community in music, the arts, movies, festivals?

- What opportunities are there for you to stand with the victims of racism, adding your voice to those protesting injustice, at school board meetings, city council hearings, court proceedings, public vigils? As a white male in our society, I am the beneficiary of many privileges, some of which are at the expense of women and people of color. Am I willing to stand with those who are denied them?

- What could you read to deepen your understanding of racism and the positive contributions of people of color to poetry, fiction, drama, political and social analysis? One especially helpful resource is Rev. Ben Chavis's three-page weekly *Civil Rights Journal*. It gives me a short regular look at issues facing people of color in the U.S. and around the world.[82]*

When considering long lists of action possibilities like this the point is not to see how many things we can do. Rather, it is to set out on a journey one step at a time that will make us into different persons and a different community.

Consequences

As the stories of Archbishop Hunthausen, Shelley and Jim Douglass, Martin Luther King, Gandhi, Ben Chavis, and so many others illustrate, peacemakers and disciples who get involved in resistance pay a price. But what they get and who they become for others make the price worth it.

Persecution: Matthew 5:10–12, 38–48; Romans 12:14–21; Luke 21:8–19; Hebrews 10:32–36; John 15:18–21, and many other passages make it abundantly clear that those of us who embrace the Word of God and dare to be disciples of Jesus will face the same fate as our Lord and friend — persecution by the world. Sometimes it will be for our resistance to the Powers and Principalities of this world. Other times it will be because we dare to stand with or even be associated with others who are victims (Heb. 10:33). Paul tells the Ephesians not to be surprised or discouraged about his imprisonment. Anyone willing to confront the Powers and Principalities should be prepared to become "a prisoner for Christ Jesus." Because we are a part of the realization of God's great mystery for the world, "we are bold enough to approach God in complete confidence, through our faith in God; so, I beg you, never lose confidence just because of the trials that I go through on your account; they are your glory" (Eph. 3:1–13). As a friend once said to me, "Bridge-builders as well as bridges should expect to get walked on."

Fruit That Will Last: "If the seed falls into the ground and dies, it will bear much fruit" (John 12:24). "I chose you and I commissioned you to go out and bear fruit, fruit that will last" (John 15:16). "I am the vine and you are the branches. Whoever remains in me, with me in them, they will bear fruit in plenty" (John 15:5). God calls us to fidelity, not to success. Gandhi spoke of "renunciation of the fruits of our actions." But if we remain faithful to daily deeds of reconciliation and resistance, the fruit will follow in its own time.

Joy: "I have told you this so that my own joy may be in you and your joy be complete" (John 15:11). Not a painless joy, but a deep abiding joy, one in which we know that the pain, united with Jesus' painful sacrifice, is redemptive.

Light and Water: "If you do away with the yoke, the clenched fist, the wicked word; if you give your bread to the hungry..., your light will rise in the darkness and your shadows become like noon. Adonai will always guide you, giving you relief in desert places. And you shall be like a watered garden, like a spring of water whose waters never run dry" (Isa. 58:10–11). God promises to be with us with an almost unbelievable intimacy (see Psalm 139). And in this process, we become an undying spring of water for others. Such an image to a desert people says how special we will become for others.

For Reflection

1. Do you feel God has called you to be a "sentry" for a portion of God's people? If so, who are the people you feel most responsible for or capable of alerting? What do you think God wants you to say to them? Recall the first chapter of Jeremiah, where God answered the reluctance to accept a prophetic call by saying to "go now to those to whom I send you and say whatever I command you."

2. God said to Jeremiah (and to us): "So now brace yourself for action....I, for my part, today will make you into a fortified city, a pillar of iron, and a wall of bronze to confront all this land....They will fight against you but shall not overcome you, for I am with you to deliver you — it is Adonai who speaks" (1:17–19). What is God saying to us here, in Acts 4:13–22 and 5:22–24 (the apostles' early experience with nonviolent resistance and its consequences), and in John 2:13–17 (Jesus' encounter with the money-changers in the temple)?

3. You can't focus on every issue and keep your sanity or integrity. In this chapter, we have looked at several idols that need confronting. Which do you feel most able to confront — militarism, racism, materialism, technologism, nationalism? What do you see as next steps in resisting the dragons of our time?

4. Even if you did not identify racism as your priority issue, is there among the suggestions above (see pp. 123–124) a step you could take to address this issue?

5. Take time to reflect on the consequences for resisters. The biblical readings are rich.

6. What support system do you have for moving further into resistance and prophetic discipleship? Are there steps you could take to increase its effectiveness?

7. Henri Nouwen writes, "Those who resist the power of

death are called to search for life always and everywhere. The search for this tender and vulnerable life is the mark of the true resister." In what ways are you already affirming life, in addition to your resistance to violence and injustice? Is there something else you want to do?

Chapter 11

Accepting and Testing Our Limits

"I don't know how you do it," a friend confessed recently, "how you keep going, in the face of all these problems. The more I see, the more overwhelmed I feel." As I absorbed what Mary was saying, another Mary came to mind, Mary the mother of Jesus. I have often thought of how she must have felt standing at the foot of the cross on which her son was dying. What could she do to relieve his suffering? How could she keep looking? In India I was struck that so many of the cars of the rich had shades on the back windows — so that those being chauffeured around wouldn't have to see the misery on the streets and be accosted by the suffering masses. They couldn't stand to see. "Lord, that I may see," I have often prayed, when tempted to shut my eyes to the suffering around me.

As I go through my mail, there is always a stack of newsletters with appeals for letters to political leaders on behalf of a variety of urgent issues. Sometimes I feel like throwing my hands up in the air and saying, "I can't deal with all this!" Now that I have begun to allow the pain and struggles of people right around me to enter my soul, in the nursing homes and shelters especially, it's getting worse in one sense. How to deal with our limits is a very real concern to everyone engaged in peacemaking.

Accepting Our Limits

Prioritize

I can't learn it all, do it all. I have to pick the issues to concentrate on, do as good a job on them as I can, and leave the other issues to other persons. This involves a process of discernment. What do I enjoy working on? What is urgent? What has my training and background best prepared me for? What integrates best with my current responsibilities, tasks, living situation? When our children were small and we were searching for a way of being of direct service to others, we thought about prison visitation and even talked with a friend in prison ministry. But we also realized our children (then one, three, and five) could not easily relate to this and we wanted the whole family to participate. So Kathy and I decided to open our home to teens needing temporary shelter and personal nurturing. Our children could relate to this and did. But a decade later we were saying no to all such requests, because our children's needs were much more complex and we didn't have the energy to deal with additional teenagers. Do I feel guilty about saying no? No, because we have accepted our limits. We have spread the word in our speaking and writing about such hospitality and have helped to find others to take on this work.

Encourage Others

Others have taken on the issues that I cannot make a priority. I pray for them and I look for ways to encourage them. That is how I can help. I have been part of groups that have divided up the issues we all wanted to address but couldn't as individuals. So we each take responsibility for one or two issues, deal with them as best we can, and share our activity with one another. At monthly meetings we have shared what we are doing and how the rest of the group could relate to our issues. At our Institute, we divide the political letter-writing responsibility and invite one another to co-sign our letters. Occasionally when I read of some courageous effort or hear that someone is paying a price for their unpopular stand, I send a note of encouragement, knowing there is no way I could be as involved in that issue. We write letters to those we want to challenge for their bad actions or policies. Why not affirm those who risk doing good?

Pray

On my "solidarity days" I pray for specific people in the struggle. I "accompany" them that day, and try to let them know of my love and support — by a letter or phone call. But I also pray to become more aware that Jesus is the Lord of history and is ultimately the one in charge, the one through whose Spirit personal conversion and social transformation take place. I am an instrument of that Spirit of compassion and have a role to play, but that work will go on without me.

And like Mary at the foot of the cross, I feel at times that there is nothing else I can do. Often when I read an account of someone imprisoned or harassed, I immediately write a postcard. But there are times when I cannot respond or do not know how to respond. At those times I try to keep the window shades of my heart up, take in the suffering, and lift it up to God. I beg God to intervene through other channels of love. I also pray that if there is something I can do, God will help me find it. There are times, in the nursing home especially, when all I can do is just be there with persons in their suffering. I use my hands a lot — holding hands, blessing them, tracing a cross on their forehead and reminding them of God's love. Sometimes when we are at a loss for words, it is not words that are needed anyway. I am learning to be content with just being there and loving with my eyes and my hands.

Acknowledge Our Sinfulness

And sometimes I don't respond, not because of principle, but because I am selfish and sinful. I'd rather be doing something else, whether my work, other projects I'm attached to, or nothing at all. And so I confess my sinfulness, ask for forgiveness, and remember how Jesus accepted his disciples that "first day back on the job" after they deserted him in his agony and death. "Peace be with you, Jim."

In Gandhi's first legal case after returning from England, where his family had invested all their resources to help him succeed for the whole family, Gandhi panicked. It was a simple matter of reading a legal brief, but he couldn't even do that. He was speechless and walked out of the court room humiliated. Shortly afterward he left for South Africa with his uncle. He was running away from his failure. I always find this story comforting when I run up against my own failures and sinfulness. *Gandhi became Gandhi.* We are in this for a lifetime. We don't have to do it all in one month or year. We will fall, but we can get up again and go on. This is one of the reasons why I like "the stations of the Cross" — to be reminded of Jesus' own falling under the weight of the cross and getting up again. It is this Jesus who breaks through our locked doors of fear, extends his forgiveness and peace, and invites us to go on, not alone but with him at our side — or even closer: "make your home in me as I make mine in you" (John 15:4).

Testing Our Limits

Gandhi became Gandhi. Francis became Francis. Dorothy Day became Dorothy Day. One reason Gandhi's life is so attractive to me was his commitment to "experiment with truth." "I have not the shadow of a doubt," he said, "that any man or woman can achieve what I have, if he or she would make the same effort and cultivate the same hope and faith."

Four Key Ingredients

I have often asked people, as I have asked you, to trace their personal histories and identify those moments that have led them to where they are today. When I have asked them to categorize what they have listed, four themes have consistently emerged. They have all been touched by human suffering, by victims of violence and injustice. They have been touched by the witness of courageous and compassionate disciples. They have felt somehow called by God and have experienced God's love and providence in their lives. And they have had communities of faith at various times in their lives that have nurtured and supported them. My own history reveals the same four ingredients.

To be touched by human suffering and roused out of my complacency, over the years, I have corresponded with a prisoner, stayed in touch with the family of another prisoner, served meals at the Catholic Worker house, done the "stations in the city" with my family and other families, gone to Nicaragua and Dachau and the Altiplano in Peru, read newsletters, visited Native American reservations as we travelled West. I don't mean to impress you with my travelog or imply that you should do likewise, but only to suggest possibilities for you.

I have already mentioned stories and biographies of *courageous disciples*. I introduced you also to Jim and Shelley Douglass. I make sure I visit with them whenever we go to Seattle, because they challenge my limits, invite me to continue my experiments with truth, and inspire me to do so. Their writings are available to you, even if you do not have opportunities to be with them personally. But you have to identify persons who will have the same effect on you. For some years I felt guilty around the Douglasses because I was not where they were. Somehow I felt I should be able to do what they are doing. Fortunately I've gotten beyond this need to copy. God has a unique ministry for each of us.

Mother of the Year is a video presentation of the inspiring story of Ruth Youngdall Nelson, a Lutheran grandmother from a well-known political family in Minnesota. At age seventy, she was voted U.S. "national mother of the year." This is the story of how she became who she was, how she raised her children to be compassionate and courageous, how they are raising their own children, and how she has continued her prophetic activities in her grandmother years — including protests against the Trident Submarine. Ruth's life can inspire in us a willingness to risk.[83*] Whether or not you follow through on this resource, consider other videos and books as an excellent way of providing the inspiration we all need to take next steps in our journeys.[84*]

My Journey as Francis the Clown

I have mentioned that my journey ran into a brick wall a couple of years ago. At the end of Christmas vacation I did not have the resources even to get out of bed in the morning and face the day. For two months I struggled with my inability to cope with almost everything. I had worked non-stop for twenty years, sixteen of them as director of our Institute. I was and still am a "workaholic." I have wonderful people in my life who help me in many ways. I know my weaknesses (with most of us, our assets are also often our liabilities). I try to take care of myself. I had done what I have suggested you do: I had worked out an ongoing formation program over the long haul that allowed me to take care of myself even as I test my limits. Still I crashed. There is much that emerged from this experience that is beautiful, much more than I can share here. But I am able to share something.

First, do take care of yourself. Find those sources of joy and recharging that can sustain you over the long haul. During those dark months leading out of the tunnel, the following were especially important for me: a "soul brother"; a musical instrument I could learn and enjoy quickly (for me it was a recorder); novel reading by a fire during winter months; candle-light dinners with Kathy; a dog I could relate to and walk daily; racquetball once a week; morning walks; popcorn and movies; visits to the Japanese Garden; journaling; NCAA basketball on TV; time to enjoy my friends. I needed to build into my life a "sabbatical" way of thinking and "mini-sabbaticals" into my daily and weekly routine. I also desperately needed a longer sabbatical, which I was able to get a year later.

I saw the three-month sabbatical I was to get as an opportunity not just to unwind, but also to test my limits. With the help of my local spiritual director and Richard Rohr, a "soul brother" some distance away, I got in touch with those areas of my life needing nurture. I felt the need to become a more spontaneous person, a more compassionate person, a person more willing and able to be bold in public, a person more enjoyable to be with, a more prayerful person. What combination of experiences could provide all that, I wondered. Where it came from, I don't know, but at some point I realized that clowning might be the way to accomplish all this.

I was not finding the time or willingness to become more a part of the daily struggles of people around me, whether at work, among family and friends, or in the community. I visited my father-in-law in a local nursing home, but had never found the desire or will to visit others. But as a clown I could. Clowns do that. They cheer people up. As Francis the Clown, I had "permission" to become compassionate. Actually it was more like a mandate. How could I claim to be a clown and not be present to others? That's the essence of being a clown, in fact — total availability. I cannot not be present to people, once I put the costume and make-up on. And besides, I have taken on the character of "Francis." The white make-up symbolizes the "every person" that a clown becomes. As I put the white face on, I am reminded that I have become all persons (talk about experiments with "oneness"!). "The secret of clowns is that in our heart, we carry every heart," one clown told me.

I have added a variety of hearts to my costume. Each one is a "magic button." Press it and you get a surprise. Press the heart on my chest and you get hugged. Press the ones on my hands and you get a shoulder rub. The ones on my shoes get you danced with. The one on my face gets you a smile. You probably don't have to go to such lengths, but I do. I have chosen a nursing home and two shelters, friends on their birthdays and when they are hurting, and walking the streets as opportunities to experiment with sharing my heart(s). How do you nurture your own compassion? Is there anything in my example that suggests possibilities for you?

I also felt a deficiency in courage. I mentioned earlier my fears about leafletting and wearing the black armband at my National Guard meetings. Despite all my public speaking, I still found myself reluctant to act more boldly in public, to "sound the trumpet" and warn the people, as Ezekiel put it. The anonymity of the clown has helped me break through internal barriers, become "outrageous" in public — walking the streets, performing spontaneously in shopping malls, the zoo, and parks, joining demonstrations and inviting passers-by to take leaflets. Francis is converting Jim.

Both as an "earth lover" and as a compulsive, I always feel a little guilty walking past litter without picking it up. I thought about carrying a litter bag around with me when I walked, but I could never find the courage to do so. What would people think if they saw me picking up trash? I decided to confront this limitation of courage as Francis the Clown and began carrying a plastic grocery bag with me whenever I would be walking the streets. I began using it in my clown routines in schools, calling it a "magic bag." If we have love in our hearts and a magic bag in our pockets, we can work magic on the earth. We can turn a polluted earth into a cleaner, more beautiful earth. After a couple of weeks of working magic on the earth as Francis, I found I was able to do the same magic as Jim. Now I carry one of those "magic bags" in my pocket as I walk in the morning. It's a practical way to integrate loving the earth into my daily routine, as well as a way of overcoming my self-consciousness. And you don't have to be a clown to use your own "magic bag."

One of the interesting discoveries Kathy and I made on our trip to India in 1972 was how "Gandhian schools" were organized. The elementary and secondary schools all had a thirty-minute period of public performance every day. Primary grades, middle grades, and junior high each had separate assemblies daily during which the children sang, read poetry, played a musical instrument, danced. Gandhi wanted a whole nation capable of "going public." Fear was the biggest obstacle as he tried to mobilize the whole nation in its liberation struggle.

For Gandhi, liberation involved a twofold struggle — political freedom from the British and internal freedom from fear. "Fearlessness" is a virtue that is generally discussed in the context of political freedom, but it is much more than a political virtue for Gandhi, just as political freedom is rooted in a deeper inner freedom. Fearlessness means freedom from all external fear, that is, fear of disease, bodily injury, and death, fear of losing one's possessions or one's loved ones, and fear of losing one's reputation or giving offense.

Gandhi felt strongly the need in nonviolent training to overcome the fear of death and the reluctance to sacrifice one's all for the sake of the cause. "If *swaraj* [political independence] is delayed, it is because we are not prepared calmly to meet death and inconvenience less than death."[85] For Gandhi, it is only when we have detached ourselves from personal desires, the ultimate of which is clinging to bodily existence, and have surrendered ourselves to God that we can say we are fearless and free. It seems clear to me that peacemakers have to prepare for the ultimate laying down of our lives by those "daily dyings" we have focused on in this book — fasting, other experiments in self-denial, service of others.

Are there ways you can experiment with "going public"? Do you wear a peace button or other symbol that expresses your values? What about bumper stickers or house signs? We have these available at the office, should you be interested and need direction.

The third limit I am testing through clowning is spontaneity. How able am I to stop what I am doing and be really present to someone who suddenly needs me? Not very. How able am I to adjust my own agenda and focus on someone's else's? Hardly at all. I want to be in control, as a parent, as a teacher, as director. Clowning is helping me learn how to read where others are and adjust my "routines" to their needs — responding to their responses and creating something quite different from what I had intended. That's hard for me to learn, but it is paying off in my "other life." Again, Francis is converting Jim. Is this an area in which you need to experiment? Are you a person who needs to be in control too?

Doug Hunneke, a Presbyterian pastor in Northern California, conducted research on three hundred rescuers of Jews during the Holocaust. His conclusions provide important principles for people involved in "formation," whether our own personal forma-

tion process or that of others with whom we are working. He was
able to identify nine characteristics common to all three hundred
rescuers, all of which can be learned.[86] The characteristic that
most intrigued me was public performance. These rescuers were
spontaneous on their feet, able to talk their way out of tight situations, probably because they all had some experience in drama
in their youth, not necessarily formal training, but all were somehow involved in public performance.

I have often experienced in dialogues with people with whom
I disagree or in negotiations with others (including my children)
the need to be able to think creatively, to adjust my arguments
or agenda. Clowning is just one way of developing these skills.
Do you feel a need to grow in this area? What might your next
step be?

My fourth reason for clowning is to become more fun to be
with. I am generally much too serious. As Kathy reminds me
periodically, it is joyful peacemakers and disciples who will at-
tract others. If people encounter us as always grim, burdened by
too much to do and never enough time to do it, not available
for others (and even if we are physically available, our minds
and hearts are preoccupied), they won't stay around long. You
may also feel the need to "lighten up" a little. What are your
sources of joy? What are next steps for you? If you want to try
clowning, it's not hard. I found a person in clown ministry who
teaches a five-session course through the continuing education
program of our community college system. I took the five ses-
sions and learned how to make myself up, developed a costume
and character, and got the chance to practice a little. The rest is
"on-the-job training."

A Vow of Nonviolence

Vows are another way to test our limits. Catholics are perhaps
more familiar with vows than other Christians, but vows are
part of the common Christian tradition, for example, baptismal
vows and marriage vows. Vows are also part of the Jewish tradition. When the people of Israel needed God's special help,
they often took a temporary vow, accompanied by offerings and
acts of self-denial. Psalm 65 says, "I will go into your house
with . . . offerings. I will pay thee my vows."

Gandhi and Vows

Gandhi spoke of two kinds of vows. One was a private vow to help a person overcome attachment to a particular desire. The second was a public vow to resist injustice. It is critical to think about both types because there are real assaults on fidelity in our affluent society. Fidelity is an "endangered species," whether we are talking about fidelity to our partner in marriage, to our children, to our other commitments. Novelty is "in"; fidelity is "out." When Gandhi wrote the following in 1906, he had just made his vow to live a life of celibacy (*"brahmacharya"*), after six years of observing it only "willy-nilly," to use his phrase.

> The importance of vows grew upon me more clearly than ever before. I realized that a vow, far from closing the door to real freedom, opened it. Up to this time I had not met with success because the will had been lacking, because I had no faith in myself, no faith in the grace of God, and therefore, my mind had been tossed on the boisterous sea of doubts. I realized that in refusing to take a vow, a person was drawn into temptation, and that to be bound by a vow was like a passage from libertinism to a real monogamous marriage. "I believe in effort, I do not want to bind myself with vows," is the mentality of weakness and betrays a subtle desire for the thing to be avoided.... The fact, therefore, that I could rest content with an effort only, means that I have not yet clearly realized the necessity of definite action. "But supposing my views are changed in the future, how can I bind myself by a vow?" Such a doubt often deters us. But that doubt also betrays a lack of clear perception that a particular thing must be renounced.[87]

For Gandhi, vows do not limit freedom, but make freedom possible. By moving persons beyond mere "effort" to a real act of "will," a vow enables them to control their desires, to achieve the renunciation without which neither fearlessness nor freedom is possible. Vows help us in difficult periods to overcome weaknesses and temptation. They sustain commitment, which is the essence of freedom understood as surrender.

This additional power conveyed by a vow to overcome weakness seems to be due to the vow's invasion and mobilization, as it were, of the total person. Once the total person — our thoughts, desires, attitudes, words, deeds — is engaged, a greater staying power is present. A vow so engages the total person. The integrity of thought, word, and deed in Gandhi's life, from which was derived his great power, was in part due to his vows. Proclamation places an additional binding force on our decisions. A vow gives us power over ourselves and also has a powerful effect on those who are witness.

To the argument that vows prevent changing one's views, Gandhi's answer — that such doubt "betrays a lack of clear perception that a particular thing must be renounced" — raises the point of the necessity of such a "clear perception" before a vow is taken. A vow is in support of what a person clearly perceives to be truth, not just opinion. Genuine decision follows knowledge. Freedom is commitment to truth, total surrender to Truth, which is God. A vow adds the note of totality to the surrender.

Pax Christi's Vow of Nonviolence

Pax Christi USA invites us to a vow of nonviolence as a step along what they call our "journey toward disarming the heart." Our hearts as well as the nuclear arsenals of nations need disarming. Pax Christi expresses the importance of the vow of nonviolence this way:

> The nuclear age has brought us to a "new moment" — this is the challenge issued by the U.S. Catholic bishops in their peace pastoral. For the first time in history, nations have armed themselves with nuclear weapons that threaten the future of humankind. This new kind of violence demands that we evaluate war with "an entirely new attitude." Many Christians, having made this evaluation, seek to make a total break with violence. Pax Christi USA is inviting Christians who have recognized this "new moment" to take a Vow of Nonviolence. Such a gesture signifies an explicit rejection of violence and a turning toward unconditional love.

In their commentary, they write that "this is a private vow, a personal commitment. It would not be regulated by authority or carry any canonical obligation. These private, devotional vows have a solid base in tradition — they have been taken by Christians for centuries. The vow is meant to be freedom — not to be a burden of guilt. So we should begin with a thorough consideration of our readiness for the vow. We should realize that the vow implies a process toward a goal, not an overnight attainment of perfection." With Gandhi, they claim that "the vow can be a channel of grace supporting and strengthening commitment to nonviolence. It may move others to consider more deeply the Gospel teaching on nonviolence." In terms of permanence, Pax Christi says its vow is a promise that "can be made for a specified time, perhaps a year. It may be renewed annually. Some, however, may wish to make a lifetime commitment." The vow itself follows:

VOW OF NONVIOLENCE

Recognizing the violence in my own heart, yet trusting in the goodness and mercy of God, I vow for one year to practice the nonviolence of Jesus who taught us in the Sermon on the Mount: "Blessed are the peacemakers, for they shall be called the sons and daughters of God.... You have learned how it was said, 'You must love your neighbor and hate your enemy,' but I say to you, 'Love your enemies, and pray for those who persecute you. In this way, you will be daughters and sons of your Creator in heaven.'"

Before God the Creator and the Sanctifying Spirit, I vow to carry out in my life the love and example of Jesus:

- *by striving for peace within myself and seeking to be a peacemaker in my daily life;*

- *by accepting suffering rather than inflicting it;*

- *by refusing to retaliate in the face of provocation and violence;*

- *by persevering in nonviolence of tongue and heart;*

- *by living conscientiously and simply so that I do not deprive others of the means to live;*

- *by actively resisting evil and working nonviolently to abolish war and the causes of war from my own heart and from the face of the earth.*

God, I trust in your sustaining love and believe that just as you gave me the grace and desire to offer this, so you will also bestow abundant grace to fulfill it.

Pax Christi suggests preparing for the vow, taking it, and renewing it with others. They also recommend using the special peacemaking dates and seasons noted in chapter 5 (see p. 57 above), not only for taking the vow initially and marking its anniversary, but for focusing it regularly. I find it important to set aside a day each month for special consideration of the vow, with a regular time each week for rereading it.[88]

•

Now that we have come to the end of our journey together, I feel a little sad that it's over. But only this stage is over. We both have a lot of journeying still to do. It's comforting to realize how many others are on this journey with us — people we know personally, others we read about, and that great "cloud of witnesses" who have gone before us. And it's challenging to realize how many others depend on us, on our fidelity to our journey. Faithful to the children in our lives, to the people and tasks in our community, at work, around the world, our ripples go out much further than we could ever guess. Up close our experiments with truth, our journey into compassion, can seem very ordinary most of the time. But deep down the ordinary can become extraordinary. We are "one body" and affect one another and the whole "body" in our every choice. We are in this together and for the long haul. So I promise to keep you in my prayers, especially on my "solidarity days." I ask for yours. "Fling your gifts into the world!" Shalom!

Notes

1. Throughout the book I offer resources directly from me or the Institute for Peace and Justice. Contact me at the Institute, 4144 Lindell Blvd., Room 122, St. Louis, MO 63108; 314-533-4445. When the resources offered are free, please include a self-addressed, stamped envelope with your request.

2. We have an ecumenical retreat team at the Institute, a mixture of men and women, lay and clergy. If you are interested in one of our retreats for your group, contact me or the director of our "Faith and Peacemaking Program," Ronice Branding, at the Institute. Companion resources from our Institute's "Faith and Peacemaking Program" include Ronice Branding's *Peacemaking: The Journey from Fear to Love* (Christian Board of Publication, 1987), James McGinnis's *Retreat Models on the Vow of Nonviolence* (Pax Christi, 1987), Jim Douglass's *Lightning East to West*, and Angie O'Gorman's 37-minute video cassette *Nonviolent Response to Personal Assault* (Pax Christi, 1987). Some of the themes from this book are included in a booklet for children entitled *Francis and Friends*, based on the characters I use in my clowning with children. It costs $4.00 from the Institute. Contact Pax Christi USA (348 E. 10th St., Erie, PA 16503; 814-453-4955) about its own retreat program and resources on nonviolence and peacemaking.

3. By Lois Hodrick, a Disciple of Christ missioner in Zaire, in *Maryknoll* magazine, November 1984.

4. Mary Lou Kownacki, quoting Etty Hillesum, in *Pax Christi USA Magazine*, Summer 1987. This is an excellent quarterly magazine for Christian peacemakers.

5. From "The Presence of the Living God," in *Sojourners* magazine, April 1984.

6. From *Young India*, November 5, 1931, quoted in *All Men Are Brothers: The Life and Thoughts of Mahatma Gandhi as Told in His Own Words* (Continuum), p. 118.

7. One of the best collections of essays on "transforming initiatives" — Jesus' nonviolent resistance to evil — is Walter Wink's series entitled "The Third Way," in *Sojourners* magazine, beginning in November 1986.

8. From the inspiring chapter "Loving Your Enemies" in *Strength to Love* (Fortress, 1981), pp. 41–50.

9. Ibid., pp. 42–43.

10. Mary R. Schramm, *Extravagant Love* (Augsburg Publishing House, 1987), has a chapter, "Accepting Suffering, Not Oppression," that is excellent for women struggling with this distinction between suffering love and accepting oppression and abuse. Mary's chapter is also in the Winter 1988 issue of *Pax Christi USA Magazine*.

11. Dudley Weeks, *Conflict Partnership: How to Deal Effectively with Conflicts* (TransWorld Productions, 1984), is available for $10.15 (includes mailing) from the Institute for Peace and Justice. A Zen variation of his approach to conflict and reconciliation is Thich Nhat Hanh's "Seven Steps to Reconciliation" (a two-page article in *Fellowship* Magazine, July/August 1987, excerpted from a book by this Vietnamese Zen master, poet, and peace worker, entitled *Being Peace*, available from the Fellowship of Reconciliation, Box 271, Nyack, NY 10960).

12. See both *Lightning East to West* (Sunburst Press, 1980) and *Resistance and Contemplation* (Doubleday, 1972). For the passage cited, see Pyarelal, *Mahatma Gandhi: The Last Phase*, vol. 2 (Navajivan Publishing House, 1958), p. 789.

13. Henri Nouwen's "Contemplation and Ministry" appears in *Sojourners* magazine, June 1978. Other important pieces include a series entitled "A Spirituality of Peacemaking," which appeared both in the *New Oxford Review* (1069 Kains Ave., Berkeley, CA 94706) in 1985, and in *The Lutheran*, February 5 and 19 and March 5, 1986, on the relationship between prayer and resistance. See also Eknath Easwaren's outstanding pictorial biography of Gandhi, *Gandhi the Man* (from the Fellowship of Reconciliation). His *Meditation: An Eight-Point Program* (Nilgiri Press, Box 477, Petaluma, CA 94953) is excellent. From a monastic perspective, William H. Shannon, *Seeking the Face of God*, is highly recommended. Rollo May's *The Discovery of Being* and Eric Fromm's *To Have or to Be* are primers for balancing my more activist orientation toward life and prayer. Read Tagore as well as Gandhi to keep a balance between Tagore's emphasis on beauty and Gandhi's on truth and action.

14. Quoted in *Peacemaking: Day by Day*, for January 17, p. 7. This is a rich collection of reflections on nonviolence and peacemaking, from many different sources and faith traditions, available from Pax Christi USA, 348 E. 10th St., Erie, PA 16503.

15. Walter Brueggemann, a deeply committed and insightful biblical theologian, helped me understand the prophetic role. See his *Living Toward a Vision: Biblical Reflections on Shalom* (Pilgrim, 1982), and *Prophetic Imagination* (Fortress, 1978), on what it means to be a prophet in our time. A decade ago I set aside a summer to read and pray over the Hebrew prophets. With the help of a wonderful book by J. Elliott Corbett, *Prophets on Main Street* (John Knox Press, 1979), I tried to reinterpret the writings of Isaiah, Jeremiah, Amos, Micah, and Hosea for our present moment in history. What issues would these prophets be addressing were they living in our time and what would they have said? My conclusions are included in *Educating for Peace and Justice: Religious Dimensions*, volume 3 of our three-volume *Educating for Peace and Justice* manual for teachers, available from the Institute for Peace and Justice; $14.25 per volume (includes mailing) or $37 for the three-volume set.

16. In *Resistance and Contemplation*, pp. 85–89, Jim Douglass presents a fascinating account of Gandhi's Salt March and the internal preparation for it.

17. Ibid., p. 147.

18. "Praying for the People of the Soviet Union," from the Fellowship of Reconciliation.

19. Write Evangelicals for Social Action, 712 G St., S.E., Washington, DC 20003. In the video *Faces of War*, Michael Farrell (who plays "B.J." in the M.A.S.H. series) narrates a series of seven short vignettes about people suffering and working for change in Nicaragua and El Salvador. I find working and praying in relationship to those "faces of war" very helpful. The video is produced by Project Neighbors and is available for rental from our Institute.

20. Kathy and I started the network in 1980. We have a booklet available describing various models of such prayerful family support groups.

21. The Benedictine Sisters of Erie (6101 E. Lake Rd., Erie, PA 16511) have published *Liturgy of the Hours Prayerbook* with inclusive language.

22. See note 13.

23. The Presbyterian Peacemaking Program (100 Witherspoon St., Louisville, KY 40202) has put together a pamphlet, *The Biblical Witness to Peacemaking*, with a different Scripture reading for each day of the year, organized into weekly themes. Write them or us for a copy of this useful resource.

24. If you are interested in other Advent family suggestions, see our pamphlet, *Advent Activities for Families*, available from the Institute for Peace and Justice; $1.00 (includes mailing). We have a similar booklet on family Lenten activities entitled *A Walk with Jesus*, same price. Pax Christi produces excellent materials for Advent and Lent.

25. See James and Kathleen McGinnis, *Parenting for Peace and Justice* (Orbis Books, 1981), pp. 91–92.

26. Among the best resources available on the peacemaker saints mentioned here are the following:

On **Martin Luther King**, besides his many books, particularly *Strength to Love*, there is the excellent video *Trumpet of Conscience* (which can be borrowed from our Institute); see also his *Letter from a Birmingham City Jail*.

On **Archbishop Romero**, James Brockman's biography is one of the best: *The Word Remains* (Orbis, 1982). A film on Romero is available from Paulist Productions, P.O. Box 1057, Pacific Palisades, CA 90272.

On the bombings of **Hiroshima**, John Hersey's *Hiroshima* is a classic. My two favorites books on the subject are *The Day Man Lost*, stories from the perspective of Japanese researchers and the Pacific War Research Society (available from Kodansha International, 44 Montgomery St., San Francisco, CA 94104), and Eleanor Coerr's *Sadako and the Thousand Cranes* (available from the Fellowship of Reconciliation, Box 271, Nyack, NY 10960). Paper cranes make a wonderful gift to people of all ages; see chapter 9.

On **Franz Jaegerstatter**, see Gordon Zahn's biography, *In Solitary Witness* (Holt, Rinehart & Winston, 1964), and the film *The Refusal* (available from Pax Christi USA).

On **Steve Biko**, see the moving film and video *Cry Freedom*.

On **Gandhi**, besides the film *Gandhi*, there are numerous biographies, the best of which in my opinion is Eknath Easwaren's pictorial biography, *Gandhi the Man* (available from the Fellowship of Reconciliation). Gandhi's autobiography, *My Experiments with Truth*, is well worth reading.

On **Francis**, I like Murray Bodo's *The Journey and the Dream* (St. Anthony Messenger, 1972) best of all. See also the movie/video *Brother Sun, Sister Moon*.

On **Dorothy Day**, my favorite biography is Jim Forest's *Love Is the Measure* (Paulist Press, 1986). For a collection of her writings see Robert Ellsberg, ed., *By Little and by Little: The Selected Writings of Dorothy Day* (Alfred Knopf, 1988).

On **Jean Donovan** and the other U.S. women missionaries martyred in El Salvador, Ana Carrigan's *Salvador Witness* (Ballantine, 1986) is the best written version I have found. Both the one-hour documentary *Roses in December* and the full-length film *Choices of the Heart* are outstanding audio-visual versions of their story.

A series of "contemporary icons" of these peacemakers is produced by Bridge Building Icons, 211 Park St., Burlington, VT 05401-9856. They come as prayer cards, greeting cards, posters and plaques, and make wonderful gifts.

See also *Educating for Peace and Justice: Religious Dimensions*, unit on "Today's Peacemakers," for an extensive list of books and AVs for children as well as adults on twenty contemporary peacemakers, including many of those mentioned here.

27. See his *Hymn of the Universe* (Harper & Row, 1965) and his abbreviated version in *The Critic* magazine, February/March 1965.

28. Available from the Holy Childhood Association, 1720 Massachusetts Ave., N.W., Washington, DC 20036.

29. *A Theology of Liberation* (Orbis Books, 1973), pp. 300–301.

30. Quoted by Pope Paul VI, *On the Development of Peoples*, no. 23.

31. Henri Nouwen's two-part series in *Sojourners* magazine, June and July 1981, is entitled "The Selfless Way of Christ" and "Temptation: The Pull Toward Upward Mobility." Richard Rohr presents his challenging vision and guidance through audio cassettes, available through St. Anthony Messenger. Perhaps most helpful on this topic is a series of eight that includes "Making Room for Freedom: Liberating the Affluent," "What Is the Good Life? Breaking Out of the Consumer Trap," "Leaving Security Behind: Finding a New Center," and "Surrendering: Giving Everything We Are." Jim Douglass's treatment of the temptations of Jesus (paralleling Nouwen's treatment) is in the chapter on "The Yin-Yang of Resistance and Contemplation" in *Resistance and Contemplation*.

32. Based on Cajetan Esser, O.F.M., and Engelbert Grau, O.F.M., "Life without Possessions: The Concept of Poverty According to St. Francis," a privately distributed paper, October 8, 1972.

33. All the books and videos I listed in chapter 5 (see notes 23–26) are helpful here as well. Some practical "how to do it" books and guides for individuals, families, and congregations include Doris Longacre's *Living More with Less* (Herald Press, 1980), Dieter Hessel's *Shalom Connections in Personal and Congregational Life* (from Alternatives, Ellenwood, GA 30049), and William Gibson's *A Covenant Group for Lifestyle Assessment* (from the Program Agency of the Presbyterian Church USA). A twenty-page booklet for families I co-authored with Winnie Honeywell, entitled *A Question of Balance: Families and Economic Justice*, is also available from our Institute. It incorporates reflection from both Presbyterian and Catholic documents, as well as practical action suggestions.

34. Our Parenting for Peace and Justice Network has an excellent bibliography of multicultural books for children of all ages.

35. Jon Sobrino, S.J., "The New Figure of Jesus Christ in Latin America," from CRISPAZ, 1986. See also his book on solidarity, entitled *A Theology of Christian Solidarity* (Orbis Books, 1986).

36. *I, Francis* (Orbis Books, 1982), pp. 89–90; italics mine.

37. *Teaching Peace* is recorded by Red Grammer and is available from Smilin' Atcha Music, P.O. Box 446, Chester, NY 10918; 914-469-9450.

38. From *Peaceweaving* (Pax Christi USA), Winter 1988.

39. Ram Dass, in *Grist for the Mill*, as quoted in *Peacemaking: Day by Day*, February 10.

40. "Contemplation and Ministry," *Sojourners*, June 1978, p. 12.

41. *Resistance and Contemplation* (Doubleday, 1972).

42. The scene is well depicted both in the film *Brother Sun, Sister Moon* and Murray Bodo's *The Journey and the Dream*, pp. 16–17.

43. *Young India*, April 3, 1924.

44. *Harijan*, August 29, 1936.

45. *Discourses on the Gita*, July 14, 1926, quoted in *Selected Works of Gandhi*, vol. 6, p. 126.

46. Contact the Quixote Center, P.O. Box 5206, Hyattsville, MD 20782.

47. Contact SHARE's "Going Home Campaign" at Box 24, Cardinal Station, Washington, DC 20064.

48. Subscribing to the *Letter to the Churches* provides a regular opportunity for solidarity with the people of El Salvador. Write CRISPAZ (Cristianos por la Paz en El Salvador, Box 351, San Antonio, TX 78291).

49. From the Maryknoll Missioners, Maryknoll, NY 10545.

50. From *Touch the Earth*, a beautiful anthology of the wisdom of Native Americans, compiled by T. C. McLuhan (Outerbridge & Dienstfrey, 1971), p. 6.

51. *I, Francis*, pp. 75–76.

52. See his *Sand County Almanac* (Ballantine Books, 1966), for a complete statement of his land ethic.

53. See his eloquent *The Earth Speaks* (Institute for Earth Education, P.O. Box 288, Warrenville, IL 60555), pp. 3–7.

54. "The Way to Start a Day," in *The Earth Speaks*, pp. 14–17.

55. "Hugg-A-Planet Earth" comes in three sizes — 6" diameter, $7.50; 12" diameter, $17.00; and 24" diameter, $109.00; from XTC Products, Inc., 247 Rockingstone Ave., Larchmont, NY 10538; 914-833-0200.

56. *Touch the Earth*, p. 6.

57. In *The Earth Speaks*, p. 111.

58. Ibid., p. 5.

59. For a list of "101 Things You Can Do to Promote Green Values," see *Helping Families Care* (Meyer-Stone Books and the Institute for Peace and Justice, 1989), p. 128, or write to me at the Institute.

60. If you are interested in other "whole family" ways of loving the earth, write me for a copy of the December 1988 issue of our Parenting for Peace and Justice Network Newsletter on "Loving the Earth."

61. *Christian Faith and Economic Justice*, no. 29.133–4.

62. *I, Francis*, p. 75.

63. *The Universe Is a Green Dragon* is available from Bear & Co., P.O. Drawer 2860, Santa Fe, NM 87504. Another prayerful and prophetic peacemaker who is deeply in touch with the universe and whose writings I highly recommend is Patricia Mische. See her "Toward a Global Spirituality" in *The Whole Earth Papers* (no. 16), Global Education Associates (475 Riverside Dr., New York, NY 10115).

64. As translated in a excellent book of multiracial, gender-inclusive, and creation-centered prayer services entitled *More Than Words: Prayer and Ritual for Inclusive Communities*, by Janet Schaffran and Pat Kozak (Meyer-Stone Books, 1988).

65. Write me if you would like a copy of the song in other languages as well.

66. Children seven to eighteen should contact Kids Meeting Kids Can Make a Difference (Box 8H, 380 Riverside Dr., New York, NY 10027) about a pen-pal. Adults can contact the International Friendship League (22 Batterymarch St., Boston, MA 02109; 617-523-4273) or our Parenting for Peace and Justice Network.

67. Contact the Institute for Soviet-American Relations (2738 McKinley St., N.W., Washington, DC 20015; 202-244-4725) or a local international visitors or peace group to be part of such bridge-building efforts.

68. For instructions on how to fold paper cranes, see *Helping Families Care*, p. 121, or write to me at the Institute.

69. See John E. Mack, M.D., "Research on the Impact of Nuclear Arms on Children in the USA," International Physicians for the Prevention of Nuclear War, *Forum*, Winter 1984. A powerful video portrayal, in the voices of children themselves, is *In the Nuclear Shadow: What Can the Children Tell Us?*, produced by Vivienne Verdon-Roe and available from the Educational Film and Video Project in Berkeley, Calif.

70. See Vincent Harding's "In the Company of the Faithful," a moving commentary on Hebrews 10:32–39, 11:8–13, 12:1–4, where Paul recounts the stories of the "heroes of faith" who have gone before us. This is one of a five-article publication entitled *Martin Luther King, Jr.,*

and the Company of the Faithful, 1986, 28 pages; $3.00 from *Sojourners* Magazine, P.O. Box 29272, Washington, DC 20017.

71. "A Spirituality of Peacemaking," *New Oxford Review*, October 1985.

72. Martin Luther King, "Beyond Vietnam," 1967.

73. For extensive consideration of how families can respond to all the idols and "isms" treated in this chapter, especially racism and sexism, see Kathleen and James McGinnis, *Parenting for Peace and Justice* (Orbis Books, 1980), and Kathleen McGinnis and Barbara Oehlberg, *Starting Out Right* (Meyer-Stone Books, 1988), for adults who nurture young children. For educators at all levels, all three volumes of *Educating for Peace and Justice* provide action and teaching suggestions on all these issues. For people in seminary work, there is a special section in volume 3 on "Integrating Peace and Justice into the Spiritual Life of the Seminary."

74. From a *Ground Zero* newsletter.

75. See John Kavanaugh, *Following Christ in a Consumer Society* (Orbis Books, 1981).

76. In *Renewing the Earth: Catholic Documents on Peace, Justice, and Liberation* (Doubleday Image Books, 1977), pp. 483–485.

77. A 16mm movie like *Seeing Through Commercials* (17 minutes; from Barr Films, P.O. Box 5677, Pasadena, CA 91107) is an excellent resource for parents and teachers working with grade-school-age children.

78. We have put together a guide for helping people of faith work through this issue. We do not try to convince you of any particular action but provide a process for coming to a conscientious decision. Write me at the Institute if you want a copy of this eight-page booklet.

79. Pax Christi USA publishes a small pamphlet that lists fifty-two actions for peace, one for each week of the year. Jim and Shelley Douglass's Ground Zero community and their nationwide "tracks campaign" link people of faith in resistance all along the tracks that carry nuclear weapons materials from their points of production to where they are tested and then deployed. Write them at the Ground Zero Center for Nonviolent Action, 16159 Clear Creek Rd. N.W., Poulsbo, WA 98370. Another U.S. resistance campaign that is gathering momentum and mobilizing many people of faith is the Nevada Desert Witness. This Franciscan-based group organizes year round actions at the Nevada testing site for all U.S. nuclear warheads. These are always prayerful events and some are explicitly linked with appropriate days and seasons within the liturgical year. Even if you cannot be physically present, you can spiritually accompany those who are. Write them at P.O. Box 4487, Las Vegas, NV 89127, for their newsletter. Jonah House in Baltimore is but one of the many groups involved in "Plowshares" actions to help us see the effects of nuclear warheads on our farms, cities, and sea coasts.

80. The Presbyterian Church USA has a study program entitled *Are We Called to Resistance?* "Faith and Resistance Retreats" is a program organized by Ardeth Platte, a Roman Catholic religious who has paid a price for her involvement in politics and resistance. Contact her at 903

N. 7th, Saginaw, MI 48601, or Tom Cordaro at Pax Christi USA, for further information. A forty-page guide for making individual and corporate decisions about civil disobedience from a faith perspective is *Civil Disobedience: An Old Voice in a New Age*, published by the Leadership Conference of Women Religious [Roman Catholic], 8808 Cameron St., Silver Spring, MD 20910. *The Nuclear Resister* (P.O. Box 43383, Tucson, AZ 85733) is a bimonthly newspaper describing the actions of resisters throughout the U.S., the status of their cases in court, and the addresses of those in prison.

81. See his *Christ and Violence* (Herald Press, 1979).

82. Write him at the United Church of Christ Commission for Racial Justice, 105 Madison Ave., New York, NY 10016. Other very helpful resources are two books written by Lois Stalvey. *The Education of a "WASP"* recounts the story of her own awakening as a mother concerned about the quality of her children's education in an all-white school system in suburban Omaha. Her journey eventually led to her husband's losing his job and their move to Philadelphia. *Getting Ready* follows them into the Philadelphia public school system and the difficult decisions they faced as a white family in predominantly African-American schools. Their struggles and witness have much to offer other white North Americans.

83. *Mother of the Year* is available both as a 16mm film and as a video cassette. You can rent the video cassette from our Institute. To purchase the film version, contact its producer John de Graaf (KCTS-TV, 4045 Brooklyn Ave N.E., Seattle, WA 98105). One place to rent the film version is Augsburg Publishing Co, 417 S. 4th St., Minneapolis, MN 55415; 1-800-328-4648.

84. Other appropriate videos include *Silkwood* (the story of Karen Silkwood, an "ordinary" working woman who "blew the whistle" in a nuclear plant and paid for her courage with her life), *Norma Rae* (a fictional version of actual labor organizing efforts that result in other "ordinary" persons doing extraordinary things and paying for it), *Marie* (another "whistle blower," this time a government employee involved in prisons), *Eyes on the Prize* (the PBS series on the U.S. civil rights movement), *Gandhi* (of course), and *Amazing Grace and Chuck* (the moving story of a little league baseball player who gives up this most important activity in his life as a protest against nuclear weapons). Most of these and other similar videos can be found in local video stores.

85. *Young India*, October 13, 1921.

86. See his book, *The Moses of Rovno* (Dodd, Mead and Co, 1985).

87. *Autobiography*, pp. 318, 207.

88. For further information and helpful resources on the vow, write Pax Christi USA, 348 E. 10th St., Erie, PA 16503.